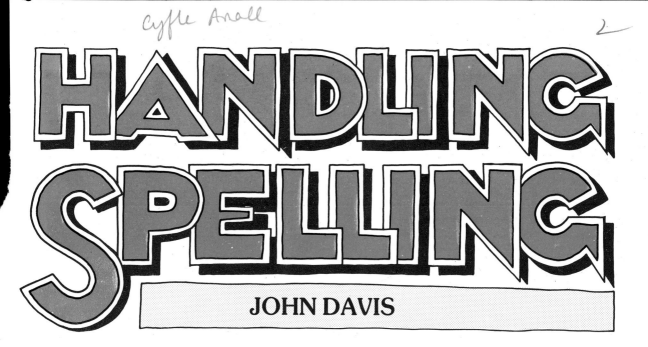

HANDLING SPELLING

JOHN DAVIS

Illustrations by John Davis
and Graham Humphreys

Stanley Thornes (Publishers) Ltd.

Originally published in 1985 by Hutchinson Education
Reprinted 1985, 1986, 1988

Reprinted in 1991 by
Stanley Thornes (Publishers) Ltd
Old Station Drive
Leckhampton
CHELTENHAM GL53 0DN

British Library Cataloguing in Publication Data

Davis, John
    Handling Spelling
    1. Spellers
    I. Title
    428.1   PE1145.2

    ISBN 0 7487 0274 1

To my daughters
Marion Ruth and Andrea Susan

Printed and bound in Great Britain at
Martin's of Berwick

CONTENTS

PREFACE

If boredom is the enemy of learning, this book has banished the enemy. The exercises and examples include no less than three hundred jokes, forty-four epigrams and metaphors, forty amusing rhymes, and twenty-three verses from the great poets.

The exercises are carefully graded in order of difficulty, ranging from simple questions that every pupil can answer, to a few difficult ones at the end.

The seventy-five illustrations and twenty-four 'mnemonic word-panels' are reinforcements of the lessons in visual terms, a unique feature being that fifty-seven of the illustrations are constructed from the actual letters dealt with in the lesson.

The lessons cover every aspect of spelling, and the variety and entertainment afforded should make the work enjoyable as well as instructive.

John Davis

Also by the same author
Handling Language 1
Handling Language 2
Handling Punctuation

WHEN TO ADD AN 'E'

The vowels

> Vowels may be sounded 'short' (as in the word 'hop') or 'long' (as in the word 'hope').
>
> | | | | | |
> |---|---|---|---|---|
> | *short* | măt | făt | bĭt | cŭt |
> | *long* | māte | fāte | bīte | cūte |

(a) What changed the short vowel ŏ in 'hŏp' into the long vowel ō in 'hōpe', was the final −e.

This −e has no sound itself (it is known as 'the silent e'); it controls the previous vowel and makes it sound 'long'.

The marks ˘(hŏp) and ‐ (hōpe) are used in dictionaries to show whether a vowel is meant to be pronounced short or long.

(b) There are some two-letter words which have a long vowel without a final − e, for example:
mē, wē, sō, gō, nō, bȳ, mȳ

Special note:
The letter 'y' may be used as a vowel. The same applies to words ending with two vowels:
too, tea, you, see, say, boy

(c) Write out the following, putting in the missing letters or words.

1 There was a young lady of Riga,
  Who rod_ with a smil_ on a tiger;
  They returned from the rid_
  With the lady insid_
  And the _____ on the face of the tiger.
2 'Sorry I'm lat_, Sir, I nearly brok_ my ankle slipping on the ic_ outsid_ my front gat_.'
  'I see. Just another lam_ excus_!'
3 'I'm tir_d of this kind of lif_. I've packed my cas_ and I'm leaving hom_ to have a good tim_!'
  'What a terrible thing to say! If your poor father was al_____, he would turn in his _____!'

(d) Write out the following, putting in the missing long vowels.

1 lemon_de	6 conf_se	11 supp_se
2 compl_te	7 arr_ve	12 fort_ne
3 enqu_re	8 sinc_re	13 advent_re
4 am_se	9 prop_se	14 wr_tes
5 rev_ve	10 inv_tes	15 l_nely

WITH 'E' ON THE END, THE VOWELS EXTEND.

> 'Why did the germ cross the microscope?'
> 'To get to the other *slide!*'

2

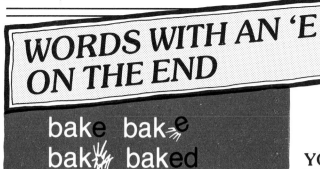

WORDS WITH AN 'E' ON THE END

bake bak~e~
bak~e~ baked

YOU TAKE OFF THE 'E' WHEN YOU ADD 'ED'.

> Words with an 'e' on the end have to drop the 'e' before adding an ending which starts with a vowel.

hope — take off the 'e' and add 'ed'
hope — take off the 'e' and add 'ing'
the correct words are **hoped** and **hoping**

(a) Write out the following, adding 'ed' or 'ing' to the unfinished words.

1 'Why are you smok_ that vile cigar in my liv_ room?'
'I might ask you the same question.'
'But I am not smok_ a cigar!'
'Well, that's why I'm not asking it.'
2 'How do you stop a bull from charg_?'
'Take away its credit card.'
3 To have friends you will keep for a long time means hav_ to spend a long time mak_ them.
4 'What's the difference between a Roman barber and an excit_ owner of a circus?'
'One is a shav_ Roman, and the other is a rav_ showman.'
5 Customer: 'Your opening sale has clos_. What happens now?'
Assistant: 'Our clos_ sale opens and everything must go, me includ_!'
6 Advertisement: 'Frantic mother wants to buy time-consum_ items with lots of nuts and bolts for small boy to destroy. Alternatively, would be prepar_ to consider trad_ small boy.'

YOU TAKE OFF THE 'E' WHEN YOU ADD 'ING'.

(b) Write out the following words, adding 'ed' and 'ing'. Set the words out in three columns as in the example given.

ache	ached	aching
1 shove	9 tease	17 place
2 care	10 move	18 make
3 pursue	11 figure	19 unite
4 centre	12 cruise	20 picture
5 loose	13 amuse	21 purchase
6 lose	14 please	22 praise
7 arrange	15 imagine	23 introduce
8 glue	16 excite	24 misuse

(c) Write out the following words, removing the endings 'ed' or 'ing', for example: behaving — behave.

misused	collapsed	advised
perusing	distributing	celebrating
colonized	besieged	investigated
seizing	believing	disobliging
determined	achieved	evaporating
practising	licenced	retrieving

> Voice: 'I *phoned* up to tell you that Jimmy won't be *coming* to school today. He's not well.'
> Teacher: 'I'm sorry to hear that. Who is speaking?'
> Voice: 'My father, Miss.'

> 'What happened to the couple that met in a *revolving* door?'
> 'They're still going around together.'

WHEN TO TAKE OFF THE 'E'

**Bite off the 'e' and so enable
the adding of suffixes like 'able'.**

RELAT**E** – RELAT**E**
RELAT**ED** : RELAT**ING**
RELAT**IVE** : RELAT**ION**

In most cases, the 'e' is removed when a suffix beginning with a *vowel* is added to the word, for example:

juice + y = juicy (the 'e' has gone)
love + able = lovable
educate + ion = education

(a) Write out each of the following words adding a *vowel* suffix. Do *not* use the suffixes '_ed' or '_ing'.
Use as many different suffixes as you can.
For example:

value — valu*able* — valu*ation*
white — whit*er* — whit*est*
imagine — imagin*ary* — imagin*ation*

translate	indicate	sincere
observe	force	secure
waste	define	compose
advise	pure	ridicule
noise	organise	invite
combine	admire	oppose
manicure	televise	prepare
complete	compare	anticipate
survive	nature	transfuse
revolve	illuminate	behave

(b) Write out the following, putting these ten words in the spaces.

1	relative	6	valuable
2	practising	7	expensive
3	opposition	8	inflation
4	nudist	9	rarest
5	elevator	10	behaviour

1 A hole was made in a fence surrounding a _____ camp.
Police are now looking into it.
2 'What did the burglar say to the watchmaker?'
'Sorry to have taken so much of your _____ time.'
3 In spite of the _____ in the economy, the wages of sin stay the same.
4 When a minister rehearses his sermon, is he _____ what he preaches?
5 A report from the Borough Council says that a new mortuary will be built, in spite of stiff _____ .
6 'I joined the firm as the _____ attendant, because I thought it would eventually get me to the top.'
7 When is roast beef very _____ ?'
'When it is at its _____ .'

(c) Write out the following words *without* their vowel suffix endings.

1	association	6	confusion
2	complication	7	introduction
3	famous	8	believable
4	assurance	9	serenity
5	mandatory	10	picturesque

Note these exceptions: unshakeable
likeable rateable saleable sizeable

'Is there a way of telling if a fellow has a glass eye?'
'No, but it could come out during the *conversation*.'

WHEN TO KEEP THE 'E'

lov **e**

love + ly

= lovely

> When a consonant suffix
> is put on the end,
> the 'e' keeps its place,
> its rights to defend.

In most cases, the 'e' stays with the word when a suffix beginning with a *consonant* is added, for example:

care + less = careless
care + ful = careful
lone + some = lonesome
lone + ly = lonely
move + ment = movement

(a) Write out the following words adding a *consonant* suffix. In some cases you may be able to provide two suffixes.

1 late	11 complete	21 like
2 age	12 arrange	22 strange
3 tire	13 atone	23 enforce
4 time	14 false	24 advertise
5 secure	15 plate	25 require
6 taste	16 hope	26 improve
7 sense	17 ripe	27 achieve
8 refine	18 use	28 displace
9 excite	19 safe	29 aggressive
10 genuine	20 life	30 assertive

(b) Write out the following, putting these eight words in the spaces.

1 replacement	5 improvement
2 engagement	6 statement
3 timely	7 safety
4 elopement	8 advertisement

1 'Weren't you hurt when you sat on that pin?'
'No, it was a _____ pin.'
2 'Have you heard that Charlie Smells is changing his name?'
'No, but any change must be an _____.'
'Yes, he's changing it to Freddie Smells.'
3 'What kind of invention was the clock? I'll tell you: a _____ one.'
4 'I'm very sorry, lady, but I've just run over your cat. Can I provide a _____?'
'Can you catch mice?'
5 Your conversation is your _____. Every time you open your mouth to make a _____ about something, you let others look into your mind.
6 'They were getting ready for a secret _____ when she decided her feelings towards him had changed, and she broke off the _____.'
'Is she returning the ring?'
'No, her feelings towards the ring haven't changed.'

Note these exceptions:

argue + ment = argument (take off the 'e')
wise — wisdom   whole — wholly
true and due — truly and duly

Special note:
Some words keep the 'e' even when a *vowel* suffix is added: these are words which end in '–ce' and '–ge'.

> 'Waiter, this soup is *tasteless!*'
> 'That's odd, sir, the chap behind you said it tasted of dish-water.'

WHEN TO KEEP THE 'Y'

The howls of the vowels clearly show, they're not allowing the 'Y' to go.

> If a suffix is added to a word which ends in a vowel followed by 'y', you must keep the 'y'.

ENJ**O**YED
ENJ**O**YMENT
ENJ**O**YABLE

(a) *Examples:*

employ	employment	employable
buoy	buoyant	buoyed
pray	prayed	prayers
survey	surveyor	surveying
joy	joyful	joyous
destroy	destroyed	destroyer

When the suffixes 'ing' or 'ish' are added to any word ending in 'y', you must keep the 'y'.

Examples:
baby + ish = babyish
forty + ish = fortyish
busy + ing = busying
steady + ing = steadying

> What did the surprised astronaut see in his frying-pan?
> An unidentified *frying* object.

(b) If the 'y' has the sound of long vowel 'i', keep the 'y' when adding 'ly' and 'ness' even when there is a consonant in front of the 'y'.

Examples:

sly	slyly	slyness
dry	dryly	dryness
shy	shyly	shyness

(c) Write out the following, putting in the missing letters.

1 'Hush! Hush! Whisper who dares, Christopher Robin is saying his pr_____.'
2 'Boy! Were you cop_____Mary's sums?' 'No, sir, just looking to see if she got mine right.'
3 Why did the chicken cross the road? To do some l_____ in the lay-by on the other side.

(d) Write out the following words, adding as many suffixes to each word as you can think of, which keep the 'y'.

convoy	grey	display
worry	tidy	carry
steady	busy	delay

(e) Note the following exceptions to the rule of keeping the 'y':

say	s<u>ai</u>d	pay	p<u>ai</u>d
lay	l<u>ai</u>d	slay	sl<u>ai</u>n
day	d<u>ai</u>ly	gay	g<u>ai</u>ety

A few short words which end in 'ie' and have 'ing' added, drop the 'e' and change the 'i' to a 'y', for example:

tie — tying   lie — lying   die — dying

> 'They're *burying* Old Bill in Shropshire tomorrow.'
> 'Oh, yes. What part?'
> 'All of him!'

WHEN TO USE 'IE' & 'EI'

PIECES OF EIGHT!

> When 'ie' is used, it usually gives the sound of long vowel 'ē'. When 'ei' is used, it usually gives the sound of long vowel 'ā' and occasionally, long vowel 'ī'.

(a) To make me sound like 'key',
You write me down 'ie',
But if the sound is 'weigh',
I'm round the other way.

To make me sound like 'key',
You write me down 'ie',
But if the sound is 'height',
You turn me round to get it right.

(b) Following the above rule, write out the following, putting in 'ie' or 'ei'.

1 I filled a small chest
   With p_ces of _ght,
   but soon had to rest
   Because of the w_ght.
2 I went to the top of the _ffel Tower,
   To see the Paris sights,
   But had to go without my friend,
   As he's afraid of h_ghts.
3 'I bel_ve you write with your right hand,
   or is it your left?'
   'N_ther: I use a pencil.'
4 Did you hear about the two blood cells?
   They loved in 'v_n'.

> Teacher to new boy: 'What a lovely accent you have!'
> 'I know, Miss, I'm Irish.'
> 'Oh, really?'
> 'No, Miss, *O'Reilly*.'

(c) The only words with 'ei' which have the sound of long vowel ī (as in 'bite') are as follows:

either	neither	Eileen
height	eiderdown	edelweiss
sleight	seismic	poltergeist
Fahrenheit	eisteddfod	kaleidoscope

The only words with 'ei' which have the sound of long vowel ā (as in 'hay') are as follows:

reign	veins	deity
feint	reins	sheikh
beige	neigh	veil
freight	reindeer	weigh
feign	neighbour	weight

(d) Write out the following, putting in the spaces suitable words which contain 'ei'.

1 'Boy! You have _____ blazer nor tie.
   Why aren't you wearing your school uniform?'
   'Because I don't feel like it, sir.'
   'I will deal with you later, along with the Headmaster!'
   'Why, sir, isn't he wearing uniform _____?'
2 'Please madam, will you wait?
   Just stand on me while I speak your _____.
   Get your coin ready for paying,
   Then stand quite still
   While I do the _____.'

> 'What do *reindeer* say before they tell you a joke?'
> 'This one will "*sleigh*" you.'

WHEN TO USE 'IE' & 'EI'

'It says, "Use i before e, except after c".'

After the letter 'c', write 'ei' to give the sound of the long vowel 'ē'.

Example:
Conceit (sounds like 'consēt')

(a) Write out the following, putting 'ei' or 'ie' in the blank spaces.

1 I used to be conc_ted but now I am perfect.
2 O what a tangled web we weave, when first we practise to dec_ve.
3 'Doctor, everyone I speak to says that I am a liar!'
 'I find that hard to bel_ve.'
4 Fr_ndships multiply joys and divide gr_fs.
5 When you lend money to a fr_nd, you do not ask for a rec_pt.
6 In scandal, as in robbery, the rec_ver is always as bad as the th_f.
7 Sigh no more, ladies,
 Ladies, sigh no more;
 Men were dec_vers ever.
8 'My husband wouldn't have a decorator in. He papered all the c_lings himself!'
 'I bet he thought it a great ach_vement.'
 'Well, he was very stuck-up about it at the time.'

9 The citizens of the bes_ged city were waiting to rec_ve news from th_r sover_gn that he had perc_ved th_r sad plight, and that he had conc_ved a plan to raise the s_ge and would soon be coming to rel_ve them.

(b) There are some words which do not have the sounds expected of them e.g.:

heifer	protein	weird
heir	hierarchy	bier (funeral)
weir	leisure	Sheila
seize	their	counterfeit

(c) There are also some words in which the letters 'ie' are given *separate* vowel sounds, for example:

quiet	alien	audience
diet	science	society
lenient	gradient	orient
transient	ingredient	medieval
anxiety	notoriety	variegated
piety	variety	experience

(d) Write out the following, putting suitable words from (b) and (c) in the spaces.

1 'Take our little son and _____ to feed the little ducks out there.'
2 'What did the bull sing to the cow? When I fall in love, it will be for "_____"!'
3 It wasn't the beer that carried him off, 'Twas the coffin the _____ took him off in.
4 Wife: 'I'm worried about your fat stomach — why don't you _____?'
 Husband: 'OK. What colour?'

Witness: 'She offered me this dud £5 note, Your Honour.'
Judge: 'Counterfeit?'
Witness: 'Yes, Your Honour, she had two.'

WHEN TO CHANGE THE 'Y' TO 'I'

If a suffix is added to a word which ends in a consonant followed by the letter 'y', the 'y' must be changed to 'i'.

(a) Write out the following, putting these words in the spaces.

parties	happiness	luxuries
allergic	married	marriage
emptiness	burial	buried

1 *Customer:* 'You're sneezing a lot. Do you have an allergy?'
   Shop-assistant: 'Yes, I think I must be _____ to my boss.'

2 'Empty vessels make the most sound,' they say. Nonsense! _____ can only produce silence.

3 Wife to husband: 'How is it that you're so old at home and so young at _____?'

4 I had just _____ a sergeant-major. As we came out of the church door, I turned to him for those first precious words with which to start our _____.
   'You're out of step!' he said.

5 The crossword-puzzle addict left instructions for his _____. His coffin was _____ six feet down and three across.

6 My old father used to say: 'Money can't buy _____, and _____ are what other people buy.'

'Doctor, my hair keeps falling out. Can you suggest anything to keep it in?'
'How about a *carrier* bag?'

APPLY : APPL⚡
APPLI–
APPLIED   APPLIES
APPLICANT   APPLICABLE
APPLIANCE   APPLICATOR
APPLICATION

Note the many suffixes possible once the letter 'y' has been changed to 'i'. Write out the following, putting words from the above box, inside the spaces.

(b) Applicants wishing to _____, will have to fill in an _____ form. This is not _____ to those who have already _____, as a special form _____ for a second-time _____.

(c) Write out what the following eight people study, for example:

An **etymologist** studies **etymology**.

1 psychologist	5 biologist
2 botanist	6 anthropologist
3 ornithologist	7 archaeologist
4 anatomist	8 pathologist

(d) Supply as many suffixes as possible to the following words; the suffixes must change the 'y' to another letter, for example:

heavy – heav**ily**, heav**iness**

1 occupy	5 ugly	9 duty
2 mercy	6 plenty	10 necessary
3 beauty	7 qualify	11 specify
4 secretary	8 weary	12 miscellany

DOUBLING THE CONSONANT

Vowels need *two* consonants for a 'squeezed-up' sound

CONSONANT AEIOU CONSONANT

A single-sound word like 'cat' needs only one consonant with a short vowel.
A double-sound word like 'cattle' (cat'tle) needs two consonants with a short vowel.

CAT
CATTLE

Write out the following, putting in the missing double consonants.

1 My father's mi_le class
While my mother's rather u_er,
So she always speaks of di_er
When my father wants his su_er.

2 'Waiter, is the fish cooked with ba_er?'
'No, madam, with bu_er.'
'Good, it's be_er cooked with bu_er than with ba_er.'

3 'Tell me, Mary, how do you know that ca_ots are good for your eyes?'
'I've never seen a ra_it wearing gla_es, Miss.'

4 The fe_ow who does not need to bo_ow,
Lives without wo_y about tomo_ow.

5 *Salesman:* 'This is a very clever pa_ot, sir; it can say, "Pre_y Po_y wants a chocolate to_ee".'
Customer: 'It sounds well educated.'
Salesman: 'Indeed, sir. It came to us straight from the Polytechnic.'

6 There were two a_les on the table, one large Cox's Orange Pi_in, and one small and ye_ow.
'Now, darlings,' Auntie said, 'I want to see who has the be_er ma_ers.'
'She has!' said the boy, taking the bi_er a_le.

7 *For sale:* Six Mi_ion Do_ar Man. £5 or nearest o_er.

8 The blades of grass sna_ed to a_ention in the freezing sti_ness.

9 At our co_i_ee meeting, we began with two plans of action, which we na_owed down to four.

10 A world-famous singer charged £10 for a le_on. 'I do give le_ons for £4,' he admi_ed, 'but I don't reco_end them.'

11 A woman left her hotel and said to a man she thought was a uniformed co_i_ionaire, 'Get me a taxi!'
The man cro_ly drew himself up to his full height and said: 'Madam! I am a co_ander in Her Majesty's Royal Navy!'
'Really?' said the woman, 'then get me a ba_leship.'

Listen to the 'squeezed-up' sounds of the short vowels.

WHEN TO DOUBLE THE CONSONANT

When adding a vowel suffix, double the last letter to give the vowel a short sound.

'We are putting in an extra letter!'

HOP + ED
HOP EXTRA LETTER ED
HOPPED

HOP + ING
HOP EXTRA LETTER ING
HOPPING

(a) When adding vowel suffixes such as: _ed, _ing, _er, _est, or _en, you must double the last letter if the vowel in the word is **short**, for example:

glăd	– glădden	
bĭg	– bĭgger	– bĭggest
travĕl	– travĕller	– travĕlling
hŏp	– hŏpped	– hŏpping

You do **not** double the last letter if the vowel is long:

hōpe	– hōped	– hōping
frāme	– frāmed	– frāming
rīde	– rīder	– rīding

(b) Note that in the case of single-sound words that end in **f, l** or **s**, these letters are usually doubled already, so that you simply add on the suffix, for example:

| puff | – puffed | – puffing |
| small | – smaller | – smallest |

'How do you keep a skunk from smelling?'
'Hold his nose.'

(c) Write out the following, putting in the missing letters.

1 'What do fleas do when they get really angry?'
'They go ho_ing mad.'

2 'Do you ever have trouble m_ing up your mind?'
'Well, yes and no.'

3 In the kitchen Kate went tri_ing,
Landing in a vat of dri_ing.
When the Red Cross came to fetch her,
Kate kept sli_ing off the stretcher.

4 *For sale:* Piano which would suit a begi_er with chi_ed legs.

5 'Someone was t_ing me that the dustmen are stri_ing again.'
'Don't talk ru_ish!'

6 The Arctic cold sto_ed us from pa_ing our dogs. Their tails were frozen stiff and would have sna_ed off if they had wa_ed them.

'Daddy, there's a black cat in the *dining*-room.'
'Never mind, they're lucky.'
'This one is. He's eaten your *dinner*!'

WHEN NOT TO DOUBLE THE CONSONANT

If a word has a short vowel followed by two consonants, just add a vowel suffix because the double consonant is already there.

end + ed = ended
end + ing = ending

jump (ends with the two consonants 'm' and 'p') add the suffix 'ing' and the word is 'jumping'

cross (ends with a double consonant) Never insult an alligator until you have **crossed** the river.

(a) Write out the following, putting two consonants in the spaces.

I work in a bank, and a ba_ing job is mostly si_ing at a desk. I spoke about it to my doctor, who told me that plenty of jo_ing in the park (ru_ing at a fast cra_ing pace) would add ten years to my life. He was right. I've been hu_ing and pu_ing away for half-a-mile, and I feel five years older already.

> 'My wife has an arresting way of making a long story short.'
> 'That's *interesting*, how does she do it?'
> 'She interrupts!'

If a word has two vowels, just add a vowel suffix without doubling the consonant, because two vowels count as a long vowel.

rain – raining   haul – hauled

(b) Write out the following, putting in the single consonant in the spaces.

1 'I know a joke about butter, but I had better not tell you or you might start sprea_ing it.'
2 People who think time is hea_ing, haven't tried sitting it out in a doctor's wai_ing room.
3 To let: Very nice fur_ished room to let overloo_ing the sea. Water in room.

(c) If you add a suffix to a word which ends in 'e', do not double the consonant, for example:

hōpe   ing   hōping

Write out the following, putting these words (all of which require only one consonant before the suffix) in the spaces.

1 writing   4 awful   7 haunting
2 rained   5 writer   8 required
3 later   6 endured

I have always loved that _____ song 'April in Paris', and one year I went there for a holiday in April. The weather was _____ and it _____ every day. _____ that year I met the _____ of the song and told him what I had _____.
  'What a pity,' he said. 'I had intended _____ "May in Paris", but the rhythm _____ two syllables.'

SYLLABLES

CU-CUM-BER

Breaking a word up into its syllables (its separate vowel sounds) helps to make long words easier to pronounce and spell.

The word *cucumber* broken up into its three syllables is 'cu-cum-ber'. *Punctuation* becomes 'punc-tu-a-tion'.

(a) Note that in the word 'punctuation', the letter 'a' sounds as a syllable. A vowel can be a syllable on its own and does not need a consonant. Consonants by themselves, however, cannot make a syllable and have to have a vowel as well.

a, e, i, o, u, and sometimes **y** are all vowels and if you count the number of vowels in a word, you can work out the syllables. Remember, of course, not to include silent 'e'.

Many words have two vowels next to each other which give one vowel sound; this means that the two vowels can give only one syllable, for example:

train   couch   steam   friend

If, however, the two-vowels are sounded separately, each one counts as a syllable, for example:

science (sci–ence) — two syllables
period (pe–ri–od) — three syllables

(b) Generally speaking, words have a stress on the first syllable of two-syllable words, for example: pen'–cil   vil'–lage

How many syllables are there in the word 'syllable'?

Here is a verse of a poem:

'Now fades the glimmering landscape on the sight,
And all the air a solemn stillness holds,
Save where the beetle wheels his droning flight,
And drowsy tinklings lull the distant folds.'

Write it out underlining the stressed syllable, and using an accent mark (´) at the end of the stressed syllable.

(c) There are some words which have the same spelling but have the stress on a different syllable because one is a noun and the other is a verb.

(a) Object (ob'–ject) used as a noun:
The car swerved to avoid an **object** in the middle of the road.
(b) Object (ob–ject') used as a verb:
The barrister rose to **object** to a question put to his witness.

(d) In a manner similar to the above, set out the following words giving:
(a) its stress used as a noun and a sentence in which it is used, and
(b) its stress used as a verb and a sentence in which it is used.

1 insert	6 conduct
2 permit	7 desert
3 contrast	8 extract
4 refuse	9 present
5 convict	10 protest

SYLLABLES

BOXER   **BOX'-ER**
                (showing stress)

RULES FOR ADDING A VOWEL SUFFIX

(a) If the accent or stress is on the **second** syllable and a vowel suffix is added, you double the consonant, for example:

begin (be–**gin**') + er   = beginner
              + ing   = beginning
admit (ad–**mit**') + ed   = admitted
              + ance = admittance

Note: This rule does not apply to words with 'l' on the end, because you double the consonant regardless of stress, for example:

marvel (**mar**'–vel) –   marvellous
enrol (en–**rol**')   –   enrolled

(b) If the accent is on the **first** syllable, do not double the consonant, for example:

limit (**li**'–mit) + ed   = limited
              + ing   = limiting
              + ation = limitation
orbit (**or**'–bit)+ ed   = orbited
              + ing   = orbiting
              + al   = orbital

(c) If the accent is in the **middle** of a three-syllable word, do not double the consonant, for example:

inhabit (in–**hab**'–it) + ed   = inhabited
                  + ing = inhabiting
                  + able = inhabitable

(d) Write out the following, adding the vowel suffixes 'ed' and 'ing' to each word, and putting a single or double consonant as appropriate, for example:

gallop + ed = galloped
gallop + ing   galloping

1 regret	12 profit	23 remit
2 listen	13 order	24 remember
3 summon	14 omit	25 prohibit
4 rebel	15 fulfil	26 control
5 differ	16 alter	27 acquit
6 abet	17 carpet	28 pocket
7 pilot	18 pivot	29 fasten
8 permit	19 transmit	30 commit
9 refit	20 benefit	31 lament
10 forget	21 market	32 abandon
11 limit	22 allot	33 disband

(e) If the second syllable has two vowels, do not double the consonant, for example:

conceal   concealed   concealing
remain   remained   remaining
repeat   repeated   repeating

Note these three exceptions:-

kidnap (kid'–nap) — kidnapped
worship (wor'–ship) — worshipped
handicap (hand'–i–cap) — handicapped

'Doctor, my baby has *swallowed* a flash-bulb and eaten the film out of my camera!'
'Don't worry, madam, keep him in a dark room tonight, and tomorrow we'll see if anything has *developed*.'

WHEN TO USE DOUBLE 'R'

'We do a double act,
Our act is quite incredible,
But only if the stress is right,
And NOT on the first syllable.'

(a) If a two-syllable word ends with 'r', and a suffix is added, keep a single 'r' if the accent (the stress) is on the **first** syllable, for example:

flatter (accent on first syllable)
What really flatters a man is that you think he is worth flattering.

(b) If the accent is on the **second** syllable, double the 'r' before adding the suffix, for example:

occur (accent on second syllable)
'Your lateness is becoming a frequent occurrence; the previous occasion occurred only two days ago.'

(c) Words which have **two vowels** followed by the letter 'r', have a single 'r' when a suffix is added, for example:

repair (two vowels 'ai')
+ _ed = repaired
+ _ing = repairing

(d) There are some two-syllable and three-syllable words which have a single or a double 'r', depending on whether the accent is on the first or second syllable, for example:

prefer   (accent on second syllable)
preferred   (changes to a double 'r' because the accent stays on the second syllable)
preference   (goes back to one 'r' because the accent has gone back to the first syllable)

(e) In the case of a four-syllable word with the accent on the third syllable, only one 'r' is needed:

defer — deferential   (def'er'**en**'tial)
differ — differential   (diff'er'**en**'tial)
prefer — preferential   (pref'er'**en**'tial)
refer — referendum   (ref'er'**en**'dum)

(f) The following words are a mixture of single and double 'r'; sort them out into two columns, the first being for single 'r' and the other for the double 'r'.

cleve_er	suffe_ing	infe_ence
confe_ed	refe_ence	confe_ing
orde_ed	dete_ed	appea_ed
occu_ence	offe_ing	diffe_ed
demu_ing	chee_ed	recu_ence
dete_ent	orde_ing	occu_ed
recu_ed	incu_ing	infe_ring
chee_ing	transfe_ed	despai_ing
incu_ed	offe_ed	appea_ance
diffe_ence	mothe_ing	ente_ed
repai_ed	recu_ing	honou_able
ente_ing	despai_ed	honou_ing
repai_ing	dete_ing	alte_ation
refe_ing	confe_ence	defe_ed
prefe_able	infe_ing	defe_ing
transfe_ence	demu_ed	transfe_ing

Two goats got into a rubbish dump and one of them found a reel of film. He chewed it all up.
'What was the film like?' asked his friend.
'Not bad,' said the first goat, 'but with all due *deference* to the film director, I must say I *preferred* the book.'

WHEN TO USE DOUBLE 'L'

'He leaves you his best wishes, but no money. He turned it all into *travellers'* cheques and took it with him!'

(a) The letter 'l' is not bothered about the accent when it comes to adding a vowel suffix to a two-syllable word, for example:

travel + ed = trave**ll**ed
travel + er = trave**ll**er
travel + ing = trave**ll**ing

(b) Write out the following, putting these words in the blank spaces:

rebellion   labelled
jeweller   rivalling
enrolling   metallic

1 'My boyfriend is a writer.'
   'Has he sold anything yet?'
   'I'll say he has. He sold all my rings to a
   _____.'

2 In a shop window there was a big trombone with the label: 'For the man who likes to make music.'
   Next to it was a shotgun _____
   'For the man who lives next door.'

3 Everybody should be allowed to rebel. A little _____ now and then is a good thing.

4 'My doctor said I needed a touch of iron, but I can't bear touching anything _____.'

5 Good nursing is important to recovery, often _____ the skills of the surgeon.

6 'I want you to enrol at evening classes.'
   'Oh, Mum, what for?'
   'So that you can get on in life. There's an old saying: "An _____ stone gathers no moss."'

(c) If there are two vowels before the final 'l', you do not double the 'l' before a vowel suffix, for example:

unveil (two vowels 'ei') add –ed =
unveiled (single letter 'l') add –ing =
unveiling (single letter 'l')

(d) Write out the following, putting a single 'l' or a double 'l' in the spaces.

1 A cannibal won the lottery first-prize of a small missionary wearing a large meda_ion. 'Thank you,' he said, 'but I would have preferred a large missionary wearing a small medal.'

2 As the two boys were talking, she swive_ed her head from side to side, like an appea_ing choc-ice girl in search of customers.

3 'I am cance_ing the sale of the house,' said the owner.
   'But it's a marve_ous house,' complained the estate-agent.
   'I'm not quarre_ing with that, but you've made it sound so good, I think I would be foo_ish to sell.'

4 *Notice:*   The hea_ing session by Mr Smith has had to be cance_ed owing to illness.

Some words ending in –al do not double the 'l' for a vowel suffix:

capital — capitalist — capitalism
fatal   — fatalist   — fatalism

> 'What's orange, and comes out of the ground at 100 mph?'
> 'A jet-*propelled* carrot!'

EXERCISES FOR DOUBLE AND SINGLE CONSONANTS

Customer: 'All I can read is the first three lines.'
Optician: 'Then you need glasses for "double vision".'

(a) Write out the following, putting single or double consonants in the spaces.

1 One icy day, as I ran for my bus, I sli_ed and fell, spi_ing everything out of my handbag. I shoved the items back in and got up. The driver had noticed, and was kee_ing the bus at the cor_er. Foo_ishly, I began to run, sli_ing and fa_ing a second time, again upse_ing the contents of my handbag. Smi_ing broadly, the driver drove away.

(b) Of the following twelve words, six have one letter 'l' and six have a double 'l'. Sort them out into two columns marked 'Double' and 'Single'.

1 fulfi_ment	7 i_egitimate
2 disi_usion	8 simi_arity
3 fearfu_ness	9 crysta_ized
4 mascu_inity	10 daffodi_
5 insta_ment	11 ho_owed
6 prope_er	12 woo_en

'What's grey and red all over?'
'An *embarrassed* elephant.'

(c) This is the same as above, but the words have single or double 'r'.

1 pa_alysis	7 a_ogant
2 cove_ing	8 appea_ing
3 ga_ulous	9 i_elevant
4 indiffe_ent	10 a_esting
5 pa_apet	11 ho_ible
6 ce_emony	12 noto_ious

PREFIX AL–L

(d) There is sometimes confusion between the prefix 'al' (only one letter 'l') and the word 'all' (two letters 'l').

Write out the following, and in the spaces put either 'all' as a separate word, or 'al' joined as a prefix.

1 'If we sing _ together, it will make an _ together better sound.'

2 'We are not yet _ ready to begin, and it is _ ready four o'clock!'

3 'Your three sons are _ so like their father, but I think the little one _ so resembles his mother.'

DOUBLE S–C

(e) The following six words are unusual because each one contains either a 'double s' twice, or a 'double c' and a 'double s'. Write them out, filling in the spaces with 'ss' or 'cc'.

a_e_ment	a_e_ory	po_e_ion
su_e_ful	a_a_inate	a_e_ible

THE 'C' THAT SOUNDS LIKE 'S'

When the letter 'c' is followed by the vowels 'e' or 'i' (and also 'y') it has the sound of 's'.

(a) If the letter 'c' is followed by the vowels 'a', 'o' or 'u', it has the sound of 'k'.
In most words that begin with 'c', it has the sound of 'k' unless the vowel that follows it is 'e', 'i' or 'y', for example:

cereal   **c**inders   **c**yclist

The same thing applies to the middle or the end of a word, for example:

can**c**el   coun**c**il   poli**c**e   jui**cy**

(b) When adding a suffix to a word which ends with 'ce' it is often necessary to keep the letter 'e' to avoid the sound of the 'c' changing to a 'k', for example:

peace becomes **peaceable**

without the 'e' the word would sound like 'pea cable'

Note also:
trace   + able = traceable
notice + able = noticeable
replace + able = replaceable

(c) When adding the suffix 'ing', the 'e' is not wanted because the 'c' stays like an 's' in front of the letter 'i', for example:

tracing   noticing   replacing

(d) The letter 'i' must be placed in front of the suffix 'ous' to prevent the 'c' sounding like 'k', for example:

pugnacity — pugnacious (otherwise the word would sound 'pugnaikus')

(e) The 'c' can also sound like 's' when it follows the letter 's', for example:

scenery   scissors   scythe

sceptre	scimitar	ascent
science	abscess	miscellaneous
disciple	discipline	descent
fascinates	resuscitate	scintillate
convalescent		phosphorescent
adolescent		obsolescent (-scence)
effervescent		reminiscent (-scence)

(f) Write out the following, taking words from above to fill the blank spaces.

1 Work _____ me; I can sit and look at it for hours.
2 _____, _____, little star,
   How I wonder what you are!
3 'Will you take me to the tenth?'
   The lift-boy nodded his assent,
   And we made the long _____.'
4 The silver _____ moon makes its slow _____ into the sea.
5 'There is no armour against fate;
   Death lays his _____ on kings;
   _____ and crown must tumble down,
   And in the dust be equal made
   With the crooked _____ and spade.'

'I'd like some soap, please.'
'Certainly, sir. *Scented*?'
'No, I'll take it with me.'

THE SOUND OF 'K'

> The sound 'k' is written as 'ck' when it follows the short vowel of a one-syllable word.

Examples: sack   stick   clock

(a) Suffixes may be added but the 'ck' spelling remains, for example:

wreck — wreckage   lick — licking

Note that the 'ck' keeps the vowels short because it has two consonants.

'What stops a jockey from being jokey?'
Answer: 'The letter "c" — see?'

'Waiter! What's the chicken like?'
'It doesn't like anything, sir.
It's dead!'

(b) This does not apply in the case of a **double** vowel word, for example: 'seek'.

Write out the following, putting these words in the spaces.

looking   crook   meek
speaking   stick   hook

'_____ of angling, did you know that a fishing-rod is nothing more than a _____, with a _____ in the shape of a _____ at one end, and a _____-_____ chap at the other?'

(c) *Note:* There are a few words ending in 'c' which change to 'ck' with a suffix, for example:

picnic   picnicked   picnicking
traffic   trafficked   trafficking

> The sound 'k' is sometimes written 'cc' as in 'accurate' ('akurate'), and sometimes as 'ch' as in 'chemist' (sounds like 'kemist').

(d) Write out the following, putting 'ck', 'cc' or 'ch' in the spaces.

1 'Police with tra_er dogs have so far failed to find a lead.'
2 In court was a cyclist a_used of peddling drugs. He was a bad _aracter.
3 You are not supposed to swim on a full stoma_, so after lunch, I always swim on my ba_.
4 I could have been an ar_aeologist, but I didn't want my career in ruins.
5 Notice in a _emist's shop:
 'We dispense with a_uracy.'
6 'Do you want a po_et calculator?'
 'No thank you, I know how many I have.'
7 Do not be afraid to take a big step if the o_asion calls for it.
 You can't cross a _asm in two jumps.

(e) *Note:* Sometimes 'cc' has the sound of 'ks' as in 'accident' (like 'aksident').

> 'My son had to give up a very successful career because of fallen arches.'
> 'Oh, he's an athlete?'
> 'No — an *architect*.'

WHEN THE 'G' NEEDS 'U'

'BE MY GUEST.
I NEED "U"!'

> A 'g' in front of 'e' 'i' or 'y' sounds like
> 'j'. To stop the 'g' sounding like 'j'
> before these letters, change the 'g' to
> 'gu', for example: 'guess' 'plague'.

(a) Write out the following, putting in
these words in the blank spaces.

guessed	vague	guilt
intrigued	fatigued	colleagues
League	guided	catalogue
Guild	undisguised	vogue
guests	guineas	

1 The driver with a _____ sense of _____
feels uncomfortable when he sees a
police car in his mirror.

2 *Circus lion to new lion just joining the
team:* 'You would have loved our last
trainer. He never worked us too hard or
let us get _____.
He _____ us with a love and dedication
that was _____.'
New lion: 'Why did he leave?'
Old lion: 'He didn't. We ate him!'

3 'You know, I _____ that your _____
from the _____ Against Cruel Sports
would like to be invited as _____ at the
party being held by the _____ for
Animal Welfare.

4 This _____ of new fashions gives details
of the latest _____, but I am _____ that
prices are given in _____ and not in
pounds.

THE 'DGE' THAT SOUNDS LIKE 'J'

'I'm Chancellor of the Exchequer,
And this box holds my budget.
Smile, and pay your taxes,
I know you don't begrudge it.'

> When there is the sound of 'j' in the
> word, use 'g' after a long vowel (stage)
> and 'dg' after a short vowel (bridge).

(a) Write out the following, putting in
these words (all of which contain 'dg') in the
blank spaces.

1 hedgehog	4 lodger	7 smudgy
2 gadget	5 cadger	8 wedged
3 judged	6 dodger	9 badger

1 The prize for the most useless _____ in
the kitchen was _____ to be won by the
lady who sent in a photo of her husband.

2 'A fellow with a little _____ moustache
came into the pub, went up to the corner
where the dart-board is _____, and
scored five-hundred!'
'You can't score five hundred!'
'He did. He threw a _____!'

3 The _____ who missed last week's rent,
is a bit of a _____. Furthermore, he's a
bit of a _____, and if he tries to _____
you for a loan to pay the rent, say 'No!'.

'PH' THAT SOUNDS LIKE 'F'

'With the right weights, you, too, can have a body like mine.'

> **In some words which have a Greek origin, the letters 'p' and 'h' are put together to make a new sound 'ph' which is the same as the sound of the letter 'f'.**

(a)　The Greek word 'phone' meant 'voice' or 'sound' and we have borrowed this to make words connected with sound, for example:　telephone

The Greek word 'graphē' meant 'writing' and this has been borrowed for words connected with writing or drawing, for example:　photograph

Write out the following, matching the letters in the first column with those in the second column to make complete words.

1	auto	phone	11	helio	phone
2	sym	etic	12	radio	phone
3	geo	graph	13	mega	graphy
4	phon	graph	14	tele	ology
5	tele	graphy	15	calli	phone
6	micro	graph	16	xylo	graph
7	para	phone	17	dicta	graph
8	seismo	phony	18	graph	grapher
9	saxo	ic	19	bio	phonic
10	graph	graph	20	phono	graphy

(b)　Here is a list of some words in which the 'ph' has the sound of 'f':

physics	physical	physicist
philately	philosophy	philanthropy
atmosphere	hemisphere	stratosphere
epitaph	cenotaph	orphanage
hyphen	siphon	typhoon
apostrophe	catastrophe	triumphant
prophet	nephew	emphasis

Use the following phrases in sentences:

1　a graphic account
2　a prophetic warning
3　autograph collecting
4　the atmospheric conditions
5　rabies, better known as hydrophobia
6　a phosphorescent glow
7　the philanthropist's generosity
8　the diphtheria epidemic
9　a phenomenon in the sky
10　the metamorphosis of a caterpillar

(c)　Rewrite the following jumbled words (all of which contain 'ph') in their correct form.

1	seaprh	5	myhnp	9	pragh
2	hesper	6	laihp	10	aeshp
3	lohxp	7	penoh	11	otoph
4	naphtele	8	nixhsp	12	muprith

(d)　Write out the following, putting 'ph' or 'f' in the spaces.

The –oenix rises from the –osphoric flames of the fiery –urnace. This –antastic –antasm is sometimes used gra–ically as a –anciful meta–or.

> **'Johnny, what is a cannibal?'**
> **'I don't know, Miss.'**
> **'Well, if you ate your mother and father, what would you be?'**
> **'An *orphan*, Miss.'**

'GH' THAT SOUNDS LIKE 'F'

Like the 'ph', the two letters 'gh' may also be used to make the sound of 'f', but only if the letters 'au' or 'ou' are in front.

Example:
**It wasn't the cough
That carried him off:
'Twas the coffin
They carried him off in.**

(a) Here are some words, rhyming with 'stuff', which have the letters 'gh' sounding like 'f':

rough	tough	slough
enough	roughage	toughness

these rhyme with 'toff' as in 'toffee':

cough	coughing	trough

these rhyme with 'craft':

laugh	laughing	laughter
draught	draughty	draughtsman

To find the sex of a hippo, tell it a joke. If it makes him **laugh** it's a male. If it makes her **laugh** it's a female.

(b) Write out the following, putting a suitable word (containing the sound of 'f' written as 'gh') in the spaces.

1 'April, April, _____ your girlish _____,
   Then, the moment after,
   Weep your girlish tears.'
2 Notice hanging on shop door:
   'Please shut this door; the streets are warm _____!'
3 'This collar's full of starchy stuff, it hurts my neck it is so _____!'
4 'Rugby makes you pant and puff, but one good thing, it makes you _____!'

'My heart is bad, my lungs are rough,
It's time to say "I've had enough!"
I'll give this up – not one more puff!'

5 A snake grows larger without any bother, it _____ its skin and grows another.
6 'I think a smoker's in the offing. Listen! I can hear him _____!'
7 Babies start crying at birth, but do not start _____ until they recognize their mothers!
8 There is still a _____ left on the village-green, but very few horses are around to drink from it.
9 'Landlord, bring me a _____ of beer, please, and close the window because it is so _____, then get me my _____ and come and join me in a game of _____!'

'Waiter, why is this chop so *tough*?'
'It's a karate chop.'

THE SOUND OF 'SH'

There are several ways of spelling the sound of 'sh' apart from 'sharp'.

(a) 'tion', as in 'action', 'relation'

Write out the following, putting these words in the spaces.

description	information	consideration
junction	station	option
attention	examination	preparation

1 'Do you believe in free will?'
   'We have to —we have no _____.'
2 'Young man, since this is _____ for your _____, do you mind my asking you to pay just a little _____?'
   'I'm paying as little as I can, sir.'
3 Ladies and gentlemen, for your _____, the train from Newtown _____ arriving at the _____ on platforms 4, 5 and 6, is coming in sideways!'
4 Notice in window of second-hand shop:
   'Mrs Smith has cast off clothing of every _____, for your _____.'

(b) 'sion', as in 'pension', 'excursion'

Nearly all words ending in 'sion' have the sound of 'zh' (as in 'television') because there is a vowel before 'sion'.

(c) 'ssion', as in 'progression'

'I do bird *impressions*.'
'Really? What do you do?'
'I eat worms.'

Write out the following words, adding 'sion' or 'ssion', as appropriate, and making alterations where necessary.

profess	transmit	success
decide	divide	provide
omit	commit	submit
repress	aggress	access
fuse	confuse	transfuse
impress	intrude	conclude
invade	depress	suppress
revise	persuade	explode
exclude	precise	tense
collide	erode	concuss

(d) 'ti', as in 'partial', 'initial'

Only a few words use 'ti' as 'sh'. Most of the longer words using 'ti' come from words ending in 'ence' or 'ance', for example:

confidential   comes from confidence
circumstantial comes from circumstance

(e) 'ci', as in 'special', 'social'

Many words use 'ci' as 'sh' and a large number come from words ending in 'ice' or 'ic' (also 'ics'), for example:

official   comes from office
sufficient   comes from suffice
electrician comes from electric
politician   comes from politics

(f) Write out the following, putting in 'ti' or 'ci' in the spaces.

'I regret the delay Mr Smith, but in your case it was essen—ial for the physi—an to consult the opti—an. I am sorry you've been waiting so long. Are you impa—ent?'
'No, nurse, I'm out-pa—ent.'

'My wife doesn't *appreciate* me. How about your wife?'
'I wouldn't know, I've never heard her *mention* your name.

WHEN TO USE 'CH' AND 'TCH'

WATCH

'CH' AND 'TCH' SOUND THE SAME AND ARE EASILY CONFUSED

(a) At the end of a single-syllable word with a short vowel, use 'tch'. If the word becomes two-syllables when a suffix is added, you keep the 'tch'.

My wife likes to **watch** tennis on the television, and I like **watching** cricket, so we compromise and the tennis is **switched** on.

(b) If there are two vowels before the 'ch' sound, you must use 'ch', for example:

speech   coach   peach   touch

(c) If there is a letter 'n' before the 'ch' sound, you must use 'ch', for example:

lunch   pinch   bench   launch

If money doesn't grow on trees, why do banks have so many **branches**?"

(d) If there is a letter 'r' before the 'ch' sound, you must use 'ch', for example:

church   torch   starch   archer

The best man toasted the bride and gave a **scorching** speech.

(e) Write out the following, putting 'ch' or 'tch' in the blank spaces.

Jack and Jill went mar_ing up the hill to fe_ a pail of water. Jack fell down, ca_ing his foot in a hole. He tried to steady himself by rea_ing out to clu_ the bran_ of a bee_ tree, but as he wren_ed at it, it broke off and he was pi_ed into a di_ and landed on his head.

(f) Write out the following, putting these words in the spaces.

ketchup   hatchet   satchel
butcher   kitchen   stretcher

Jack said he needed a _____, but Jill helped him home and sat him down in the _____. She put some brown paper on his crown, but finding no vinegar, she used tomato _____ instead. The poor chap looked a sight; it was as if a _____ had hacked at him with a _____. However, he soon felt better, and after a good wash, he got his _____ ready for school.

WHEN 'CH' SOUNDS LIKE 'SH'

There is a group of words which we have borrowed from the French in which the 'ch' has the sound of 'sh'.

Write out the following two passages, putting these words in the spaces.

1 champagne   5 brochure   9 chalet
2 chauffeur   6 Chateau   10 chassis
3 avalanche   7 schedule   11 chef
4 machinery   8 moustache

(a) The _____ Restaurant has printed a new _____ containing a _____ of prices, and announcing a _____ celebration for its retiring head _____.

(b) My _____ (who sports a trim _____) knows a great deal about engines and _____. He tells me that my car is fine, but the _____ is inclined to rust. He has serviced the car ready for my holiday to a little _____ in the Alps. I just hope we don't run into an _____ on the way.

LONG AND SHORT 'E'

(a) The sound of the short vowel ĕ is written in the following manner:

ĕ   as in bĕd
ai   as in said (sounds like 'sĕd')
ea   as in tread (sounds like 'trĕd')

Examples:
1 'And when the moon was overhead,
   Came two young lovers lately wed:
   "I am half sick of shadows," said
   The Lady of Shalott.'
2 'It's the privilege and pleasure
   That we treasure beyond measure.'

(b) The sound of the long vowel ē is usually written in the following three ways:

ee   as in seen
ea   as in flea
ie   as in piece
Also don't forget the 'silent e'. See page 1.

(c) Write out the following, putting in all the missing letters, including 'ea'.

1 'Waiter, what soup is this?'
   'It's b_ soup, sir.'
   'Never mind what it's been, I want to know what it is now.'
2 'Waiter, a mutton chop and chips, please. And Waiter, please be sure to make the chop l_.'
   'Certainly, sir. Which way?'

3 'I'm on a s_ food diet.'
   'R_? You're putting on weight.'
   'I know. I see food and I _t it.'
4 'S_ted one day at the organ,
   I was w_ry and ill at e_,
   And my fingers wandered idly
   Over the noisy keys.'
5 'Abou Ben Adhem (may his tribe inc_),
   Awoke one night from a deep dr_m of p_ce.'

(d) Write out the following, putting these words (all of which contain the long sound ē) in the spaces.

1 sweet	4 steel	7 feet
2 compete	5 repeat	8 steals
3 pities	6 athlete	9 underneath

1 'I said that my parents are in the iron and _____ business.'
   'I heard you. Your mother irons and your father _____.'
2 Everyone _____ me. I could have been an _____, but there were too many hurdles in my way and I just could not _____.
3 'Ah, fill the cup — what boots it to _____
   How time is slipping _____ our _____;
   Unborn tomorrow and dead yesterday,
   Why fret about them if today be _____!'

Here are eight, unusual long vowel 'ē' sounds; after checking the meanings in a dictionary, use them in sentences.

1 simile	4 finale	7 physique
2 epitome	5 obesity	8 oblique
3 seizure	6 protein	

'**What lies on the ground, a hundred feet in the air?**'
'A dead *centipede*!'

LONG AND SHORT 'U'

SHORT VOWEL LONG VOWEL

(a) The long vowel ū can be written in several ways, for example:

foot	clue	grew
truth	youth	prove
tomb	computer	doing

'u'-consonant-'e' (amūse minūte)

(b) Write out the following, putting the following ten words into the spaces.

view	hue	presume	true
stew	blue	lose	new
you		two	

1 'Dr Livingstone, I _____?'
2 A bride should have:
Something old, something _____,
Something borrowed, something

_____.

3 'I have had insomnia for _____ nights.'
'Take my tip and don't _____ any sleep over it.'
4 'It's _____ there are cannibals here, but there's no need for _____ to get into a _____.'
5 'Distance lends enchantment to the _____.
And robes the mountains in its azure _____.'

(c) the short vowel ŭ may also be written in several ways. Write out the following,

using the list of eight words in the same manner as for (b).

1	come	4	love	7	does
2	young	5	honey	8	suspense
3	trumpeter	6	tongue		

1 The bees are on strike. They want shorter flowers and more _____!
2 'How do you keep an idiot in _____?'
'_____ and see me tomorow and I'll tell you.'
3 'The _____ is playing too loud!'
'But he hasn't turned up yet.'
'Well tell him when he _____!'
4 'If all the world and love were _____,
And truth in every shepherd's _____,
These pretty pleasures might me move
To live with thee, and be thy _____.'

(d) As may be seen in (c), there are many words in which the letter 'o' makes the sound of short vowel ŭ. Write out the following, selecting a word from the list below, that seems to be appropriate to the sentence.

1 He has a mind like a _____; he just soaks up facts and figures.
2 Why is thirteen sometimes called a baker's _____?
3 My mother's _____ is my uncle.
4 Columbus _____ America.
5 I've got those _____ morning blues!
6 _____ Bridge is falling down.
7 I have _____ more to say to you.

Monday   nothing   sponge   brother
dozen   discovered   London

'I call my pet *Minūte*.'
'That's odd. Why *Minūte*?'
'Two reasons: one, he's tiny.'
'And the other reason?'
'He's my newt!'

THE LONG SOUND 'I'

'We look different, but we're related.'

THE LONG SOUND 'O'

The vowel 'o' gives you the sound.
The 'a' or 'e' just come along
To show that if they stick around,
You'll know the vowel 'ō' is long.

(a) Write out the following, putting these words (all of which contain the long sound ī) in the spaces.

kind	fighter	tide
either	exciting	knight
drive	type-cast	sky
night	fighting	lie
high	water-side	neither
died	smilingly	behind

1 'Here of a Sunday morning
   My love and I would _____,
   And see the coloured counties,
   And hear the larks so _____
   About us in the _____.'
2 'For ere she reached upon the _____,
   The first house by the _____,
   Singing in her song she _____,
   The Lady of Shalott.'
3 'In enterprise of martial _____,
   When there was any _____,
   He led his regiment from _____,
   He found it less _____.'
4 _____, he said, 'I could have been a
   printer, but I was afraid of getting
   _____.'
5 'I could have been _____ a golfer or a
   fencer, but I had _____ the _____ nor
   the thrust.'
6 'Did you hear of the brave Royal Air
   Force _____ _____-pilot who was
   given a knighthood?
   He got the nickname "The fly-by
   _____".'

Write out the following, putting these words (all of which contain the long sound ō) in the spaces.

roam	soaking	microscope
bureau	lowly	home
alone	shadows	wholly
own	slowly	trousseau
holy	towing	sewing

1 'My wife and I live all _____,
   In a little brown hut we call our _____.'
2 'Mid pleasures and palaces
   Though we may _____,
   Be it ever so humble,
   There's no place like _____.'
3 The fields had been _____ up the sun,
   but now the dark rain-clouds began
   _____ their _____ across the
   meadows.
4 'Why did the germ cross the _____?'
   'To get to the other slide.'
5 The bride opened the doors of the
   _____ where she was keeping her
   wedding _____, and placed some
   _____ materials inside.
6 'Heard a carol mournful, _____,
   Chanted loudly, chanted _____,
   Till her blood was frozen _____,
   And her eyes were darkened _____,
   Turned to towered Camelot.'

'I took my little dog to the flea circus,
and he *stole* the *show*!'

THE LONG SOUND 'A'

(a) As well as using 'the silent *e*' (See page 1), there are two main ways to write the sound of the long vowel 'ā':

1 'ai'   plain   remain   fail
(The 'ai' is always followed by at least one consonant)

2 'ay'   play   holiday   dismay
(The 'ay' is usually at the end of a word unless a suffix is added)

(b) Write out the following, putting suitable words using 'ai' or 'ay' in the blank spaces.

1 There was a young lady of Spain,
Who couldn't go out in the _____;
She'd lent her umbrella
To Queen Isabella,
Who wouldn't return it _____.

2 He that fights and runs _____
May turn and fight another _____:
But he that is in battle _____,
Will never rise to fight _____.

(c) Write out the following, putting these words (all of which have the long sound ā) in the spaces.

1 mate	6 steak	11 afraid
2 patience	7 weighs	12 weight
3 mail	8 grey	13 freight
4 female	9 patients	14 eight
5 great	10 crate	15 straight

> 'Here's a riddle for you, Prime Minister: How long can a king *reign* without a *brain*?'
> 'How old are you, Your Majesty?'

1 'Come in, number nine, your time is up!'
'But we've only got _____ boats, Bill.'
'Are you having trouble, number six?'

2 'What is the difference between a postage stamp and a girl?'
'One is a _____ fee, the other is a _____.'

3 'Duty-Officer, check the _____ of the _____ in that wooden _____!'
'Very well, First-_____, I'll go and do it _____ away.'

4 'What is the difference between a nightwatchman and a butcher?'
'One stays awake and the other _____ a _____.'

5 'You're looking rather _____ with worry, doctor. How's the practice going?'
'Not too _____, I'm _____. I am running out of _____.'
'Why's that?'
'I'm running out of _____!'

(d) There are several words with the sound of long ā but with different spellings. These aids should help:

wait
weight

way
weigh

pane	pain of an injury	sale	sail of a ship
tale	tail of a pig	made	maid is a girl
pale	pail in a sink	waste	waist in inches

THE SOUND OF 'ER'

(a) The spelling 'er' is the usual way of spelling the person who does something, for example:

baker   teacher   carpenter

However, there are a great many words with the sound 'er' but the spelling 'or', for example: editor, director

If you are not sure which ending is correct, take off the 'er' or 'or' and look at the word. If the word then ends in 'ct', add 'or'.

collect (this word ends in 'ct') add 'or', to give the word **collector**.

If the word ends in 'it' or 'ate':

visit   — add 'or' — visitor
imitate   (take off the 'e')
           — add 'or' — imitator

If the word ends in 'ess':

confess — add 'or' — confessor

(b) Write out the following, adding 'er' or 'or' in accordance with the above rules.

inspect	dictate	profess
employ	process	manage
calculate	station	negotiate
conduct	success	defect
operate	report	debate
possess	solicit	duplicate
educate	lecture	control
accelerate	signal	suppress
extract	inherit	export
council	refrigerate	instruct

(c) Write out the following, putting these words (all of which include the sound of 'er') in the spaces.

1 earth	6 worms	11 rumour
2 burglary	7 word	12 circle
3 nurse	8 furnish	13 custard
4 preferred	9 hearse	14 mirth
5 tempered	10 heard	15 world

1 '_____, what would it take to make you give me a kiss?'
  'Chloroform!'
2 'Waiter, call the manager. I can't eat this _____ pie!'
  'He wouldn't eat it either, sir.'
3 Did you hear the _____ about the watchmaker? He's winding up his business.
4 'Hello, Charlie, are you fishing?'
  'No. I'm sitting here drowning _____.'
5 For sale: 1950 Funeral _____.
  Body still in good condition.
6 'What is round and bad-_____?'
  'A vicious _____.'
7 The upholsterer was unable to _____ the police with details of the _____ at his factory.
8 'Laugh, and the whole _____ laughs with you,
  Weep, and you weep alone.
  For the brave old _____ must borrow its

  _____,
  And has trouble enough of its own.'
9 'Then, to all others, my smile you

  _____,
  'Love, when you spoke, gave a charm to each _____,
  Still my heart treasures the praises I

  _____,
  Long, long ago, long ago.'

'What do you give a sick *bird*?'
'Tweetment!'

THE SOUND OF 'AW'

'B-O-A-R-D, YOU IDIOT!'

(a) The spelling 'aw' is used:
1 at the end of a word (raw)
2 before a final 'n' (sawn)
3 at the end of a syllable
(law'yer, aw'ful, aw'ning)

The spelling 'au' is used:

1 at the beginning of a word
(autumn, automatic, August)
2 in front of the letters 'gh' (daughter)
3 in the middle of a syllable
(launch, sauce, laun'dry)

(b) Write out the following, putting one of these words into the spaces.

1 daughter	4 scored	7 source
2 claws	5 caught	8 nought
3 board	6 court	9 ought
		10 jaws

1 'How cheerfully he seems to grin,
How neatly spreads his _____,
And welcomes little fishes in
With gently smiling _____.'
2 'I told my little _____,
When playing darts, she _____ to
Stand much closer to the _____.
She stood much nearer,
The numbers were clearer,
But _____ was all she _____!'

3 A construction worker has been _____ in possession of stolen building materials. From a reliable _____, it is known that the police have concrete evidence to bring the suspect before the _____.

(c) Write out the following, putting in the missing letters.

Question: 'You are sailing n_th in a new boat you have just b_t. You tack f_ty degrees to starb_d, come about on to the p_t tack (thus avoiding an _kward q_tr turn) and hold that c_rse. What will be on y_r left hand?'

Answer: 'Fingers!'

(d) Write out the following, putting 'aw' or 'au' in the spaces.

1 appl_se	4 outl_	7 c_tion
2 l_nch	5 _ful	8 s_cer
3 d_ghter	6 str_berry	9 l_breaker

(e) There are some words having the sound of 'aw' which sound exactly the same but have different spellings. The following memory aids may be of help.

A BOAR IS AN ANIMAL	BORE
HOARD CASH	HORDE
A ROAR IS A NOISE	RAW
SORE THROAT	SAW

Wife: 'I saw the doctor today, and he told me I needed a month at the seaside. Where do you think I *ought* to go?'
Husband (after a long *pause*): 'To see another doctor.'

THE SOUND OF 'OW'

(a) The sound of 'ow' can be written as 'ow' or as 'ou';

The spelling 'ow' is often used at the end of a word.
The spelling 'ou' is never at the end.

(b) Write out the following, putting these words in the blank spaces.

pound	bough	flower
wound	allowed	hour
now	pronounced	grounds
about	how	mouth

1 'That's a good watch! Can I get one like it?'
   'I'm afraid not; the firm that makes it is being _____ up.'
2 '_____ doth the little busy bee
   Improve each shining _____,
   And gather honey all the day
   From every opening _____.'
3 'Woodman, spare that tree!
   Touch not a single _____!
   In youth it has protected me,
   And I'll protect it _____.'
4 There was a man who murdered both his parents, and when sentence was _____ to be _____, he pleaded for mercy on the _____ that he was an orphan.
5 A small boy had put a 50p piece in his _____ and accidentally swallowed it. The hospital doctor said that the boy would have to lose half a _____ before being _____ home.

> 'You're very small,' *growled* the elephant to the *mouse.*
> 'Well, I haven't been very well lately,' explained the rodent.

WHEN TO USE 'OY' AND 'OI'

ANNOY
        'OY' AT THE END
SPOIL
        'OI' IN THE MIDDLE

(a) Use **oy** only at the end of a word.
Use **oi** in the middle of a word.

In the case of 'oy', an added 's' or suffix will also put it in the middle of a word: **enjoying**

Four words do not have 'oy' at the end :

royal   loyal   oyster   voyage

(b) Write out the following, putting 'oy' or 'oi' in the spaces.

1 What sort of n_se ann_s an _ster, when an _ster's in a stew?
2 To take j_ in conquest is to rej_ce in the loss of human life.
3 'Sing, and the hills will answer,
   'Sigh, it is lost on the air;
   The echoes rebound to a j_ful sound,
   And shrink from v_cing care.'
4 'When a felon's not depl_ed in his empl_ment,
   Or maturing his felonious little plans.
   His capacity for innocent enj_ment
   Is just as great as any honest man's.'
5 Dear Sir,
   Please excuse my being absent for our app_ntment and accept my apologies if you were disapp_nted. I was waiting for the bus at twenty to nine, but had to go back to use the t_let and missed it.

> 'What do you put on a pig with a sore nose?'
> '*Oinkment!*'

THE SOUNDS OF 'EAR' AND 'AIR'

'I'll take a half.'
'I'm sorry, madam, but we do not split hares!'

(a) The sound of 'air' can be written:
'air' (hair)   'are' (hare)
'eir' (heir)   'ear' (bear)
'ere' (where)   'aer' (aerial)
Note: 'aero' as in aeroplane

Write out the following, putting in the missing letters.

1 'Grocer, do you have any broken biscuits?'
   'Certainly, madam.'
   'Then you should have been more c_ful.'
2 One morning I woke up and found an _oplane in my house. I had left the landing light on.
3 'What happened to the boy who slept with his head under his pillow?'
   'The f_ies took all his teeth away.'
4 'What has a ball got to do with a prince?'
   'One is h_ to the throne, and the other is thrown into the _.'
5 'When I sat down to play the piano, everyone laughed at me.'
   'Why did they do that?'
   'Th_ wasn't a ch_!'
6 As I walk along the Bois-Boo-Long
   With an independent _____,
   You can hear the girls de_,
   'He must be a million_!'

7 'Rings are round, but I know one that is sq_ in _rea.'
   'So do I – a boxing ring.'

(b) The sound of 'ear' can be written:

'ear' (fear)   'eer' (steer)
'ere' (here)   'ier' (bier)

Write out the following, putting in the missing letters.

1 Notice in a jeweller's shop:
   'Ears p_ while you wait.'
2 'Why is a theatre a sad place?'
   'Because the seats are always in t_!'
3 'Who is this? and what is h_,
   And in the lighted palace n_
   Died the sound of royal ch_;
   And they crossed themselves for f_,
   All the knights at Camelot.'
4 'But owing, I am much disposed to f_,
   To his terrible taste for tippling,
   That highly respectable gondolier
   Could never declare with a mind sinc_
   Which of the two was his offspring d_,
   And which the Royal stripling.'
5 'Only reapers, reaping early
   In among the be_rded barley,
   Hear a song that echoes cheerly
   From the river winding cl_ly,
   Down to towered Camelot.'
6 The widow sobbed and shed a t_,
   'If only he'd not drunk so much b_,
   He wouldn't have fallen in the w_,
   And I wouldn't be following his b_.'
7 D_ Sirs,
           I sent you my h_ing-aid for repair six weeks ago, and I haven't heard a thing since.
                          Yours sinc_,
                          Brigad_ Pearce

'How many ears has Captain Kirk got?'
Three: One left, one right, and a final *frontier*!'

SILENT LETTERS 'K' AND 'N'

> Some words are difficult to spell because they contain a letter without a sound — a silent letter.

(a) Quite often they are letters which had a sound in the old days, but the word has changed so that the letter is not sounded in speech but is kept in the written word. For example, the old word for 'knife' was 'kanif', which was gradually shortened to the sound of 'knif' and later on to the **sound** of 'nife' — **written** as 'knife'.

(b) The silent 'k' is usually to be found at the beginning of a word, and is followed by the letter 'n', for example:

knack	knife	knight	knapsack
knave	knead	kneel	knuckle
knitting	knot	knock	knowledge
knee	kneel	knew	know
knelt	knoll	knob	knocker

(c) Write out the following, putting 'kn' or 'n' in the spaces.

1 'Daddy, what are those holes for in this plank of wood?'
   'Those are _ot-holes.'
   'Well, if they are _ot holes, what are they?'
2 '_ock! _ock!' 'Who's there?'
   'Atch!'   'Atch who?'
   'Sorry, I didn't _ow you had a cold.'
3 I don't think much of your _ew boy-friend. He's _ock-_eed and cross-eyed – and those are his good points.
4 'Why do bakers work so hard?'
   'Because they _ead the dough.'
5 Cut the _ot to fly the flag,
   Let the bells _ell loud and clear;
   All un_own _ight comes to the field,
   To give _ocks without fear!

(d) Write out the following, putting the words 'Nott', 'knot', 'knots', 'Knotter', 'knit' or 'Knitter' in the spaces.

John Nott could not knit, so he invented a machine which could, and he called it the Nott Knitter. But the _____ _____ could not _____ _____, so he invented a machine which could _____ _____ and he called it the _____ _____. And the _____ _____ could _____ the _____ which the _____ _____ could not _____.

(e) There are a few words in which the letter 'n' is silent, usually when it follows the letter 'm', for example:

autumn	condemn	solemn
damn	column	hymn

Write out the following, putting the above words in the spaces.

'_____ the Devil,' the Parson said,
'His deeds we must _____!'
The Organist, he raised his head,
And played a loud 'Amen'.

'The _____ _____,' the Parson said,
'Is in the second _____.'
We sang our very best for him,
With voices deep and _____.

> The teacher was facing a new class.
> 'My name is Mr Smith,' he said,
> 'and I wish to be *known* as such.'
> 'Good morning, Mr Such.'

SILENT LETTERS 'H' AND 'B'

A 'w' often has a silent 'h' following it — look out!

(a) Write out the following, putting 'w' or 'wh' in the spaces.

1 The _irling leaves _ere turning cart_eels on the wind-swept lawn.
2 'I _ish I _ere _at I was _en I wanted to be _at I am now.'
3 Blessed are they _o quietly _izz around in circles, for they shall be known as '_ispering _eels'.
4 Clever is _en you believe only half of _at you hear. Brilliant is _en you know _ich half to believe.
5 '_ere do you _eigh a _ale?' 'At a _ale _eigh station.'

(b) Write out the following, putting these words (all of which contain a silent 'h') in the spaces.

heirs	khaki	wheat
honours	wharf	honouring
vehicle	whisky	dinghy

1 'The General is not going to be buried with full military _____, with his _____ _____ his memory.'
'Why ever not?'
'He's not dead yet.'
2 A garden-roller, a _____ sailing _____, five sacks of _____ and four cases of _____ have been stolen from a _____. Police are firmly convinced that the thieves used a _____ to carry off the stolen goods.

'Why do demons and *ghouls* get along so well?'
'Because demons are a *ghoul's* best friend!'

In nearly all cases, the silent 'b' follows the letter 'm' and (unless a suffix is added) it is at the end of the word.

The most important exceptions are:
debt   debtor   doubt   doubtful
subtle   subtlety   subpoena

(c) Write out the following, putting these words (all of which contain a silent 'b') in the spaces.

1 climb	3 climbing	5 plumber
2 thumbing	4 numb	6 lamb

1 Mary had a little _____, with baked potatoes and mint-sauce.
2 I could have been a _____, but that was only a pipe-dream.
3 The catkins on the branches were _____ a ride in the wind.
4 Old age is like _____ a mountain. You _____ from ledge to ledge. The higher you get, the more tired and _____ you become, but your view becomes more extensive.

'What did the biscuit say when it was run over by a bus?'
'*Crumbs!*'

THE SILENT LETTERS 'W' AND 'L'

> In most cases, the silent 'w' begins the word, and is followed by the letter 'r'.

(a) Write out the following, putting in the missing letters.

1 I could have been a sprinter, but I started off on the _ong track.
2 *For sale:* Small red-faced lady's _ist watch.
3 The tadpoles in the pond were _iggling in swarms of little black commas all _inkled up.
4 'I liked your book. _ho _ote it for you?' 'I'm so glad you liked it. Who read it to you?'
5 'A__ the front door, Johnny!' 'I can't! I didn't hear the question.'
6 Today they are _inging the bells; tomorrow they will be _inging their hands!
7 'Why don't elephants eat penguins?' They can't _ench the _appers off.'
8 The sunset _eathed Nor_ich in pale gold.
9 I have _itten an unusual murder story. The _etched victim survives a terrible ship-_eck and then gets killed by a man from another book.
10 'Mum, I don't like cheese with holes in it! Take the _ole lot away!' 'Now, don't make such a _y face! Eat the cheese and leave the holes at the side of your plate. You can feed them later to the _ens in the garden and watch them _estling and _angling to get the biggest share.'

Further examples:

wrath	awry	wreak
wraith	wrecker	wreckage
writhe	writ	writing
shipwright	wholesale	wristlet
Chiswick	Harwich	wrongdoing

'NOT A SOUND!'

> In nearly all cases, the silent 'l' is followed by the letter 'k' or the letter 'm'.

(b) Write out the following, putting in the missing letters.

1 If it were not for doctors, there wou_d be a lot more dead people w_king about.
2 'You're a very odd person!' 'T_ing to myself doesn't make me odd!' 'No, that doesn't — but you listen!'
3 Under the shady _mond tree, I hooked a sa_mon beauty. Without a qua_m, I kept quite ca_m, And went off home with my booty.
4 'Wrapped not in Eastern balms, With wisdom of the ps_ms, But with thy fleshless p_, Stretched, as if asking a_, With face as white as ch_k, With arms as thin as a st_, Go beg from other fo_k.'

> 'Really, Johnny, your *handwriting* is awful. Why don't you write more clearly?'
> 'If I did, Miss, you would be able to see my terrible spelling.'

> 'Waiter! Have you got frogs' legs?'
> 'No, sir, I always *walk* this way.'

SILENT LETTERS

(a) After the vowels 'au' or 'ou', the letters 'gh' have the sound of 'f' (see page 21) but if a letter 't' follows, the 'gh' is silent (see page 29). *For example:*

bought	brought	fought
sought	thought	nought
ought	taught	caught
naught	haughty	aught

The following are exceptions:

though	although	through
thorough	slough	sleigh
neigh	neighbour	dough

(b) Although the 'gh' is silent, when it follows the vowel 'i', it changes it from short to long.

knit (short vowel)   knight (long vowel)

Note that when 'gh' begins a word, it has the sound of hard 'g' as in the word 'ghostly'.

(c) Write out the following, putting in the missing letters.

1 'Where did you get that uns_tly black eye?'
  'I kissed the bride after the wedding.'
  'But everyone does that!'
  'Yes, but I did it a fort_t after.'
2 An honest politician is one who, when he is b_t, will stay b_t.
3 If you s_t to win the hand of the d_ter, you _t to have flattered the mother.
4 'Did you read the book you b_t at the shop thor_ly all the way thr_?'
  'No, but I read part of it all the way thr_!'

(d)   The silent letter 't'
Write out the following, putting these words in the blank spaces.

1 listen   3 fasten   5 hustle
2 hasten   4 Christmas

'How did you have this accident?'
'It was last _____. The sign said: "_____ the gate. Don't _____.
Just take care — there's no great _____.
Stop, look and _____!"', and while I was reading it, the train hit me!'

(e)   The silent letter 'p'
Write out the following, putting *psychiatrist, receipt* and *pneumatic* in the blank spaces.

1 When you lend money to a friend, you do not ask for a _____.
2 'Do you like working with a _____ drill?'
  'Oh, yes. I used to drive a school bus, but I couldn't stand the noise.'
3 A cannibal went to see a _____. He was fed up with people.

Examples of words with silent 'p':

psalm	pneumonia	pseudonym
psychic	psychologist	psychopath
raspberry	cupboard	corps

(f)   The silent letter 'g'
The silent 'g' is followed by the letter 'n', for example:

gnat	gnu gnaw gnash	
gnome	gnarled	benign
poignant	malign	assignment
design	campaign	consignment
feign	sovereign	foreign

(two exceptions: phlegm diaphragm)

Note that the silent 'g' follows the letters 'i' or 'ei'.

There was once a tiger who *caught* measles. He became so spotty, he was sent to a leopard colony.

THE PLURAL OF NOUNS

Singular comes from the word *single* and means one on its own. Plural means more than just one.

BUS + ES = BUSES
GLASS + ES = GLASSES
BOX + ES = BOXES
BRUSH + ES = BRUSHES
RANCH + ES = RANCHES
WATCH + ES = WATCHES

(a) The usual way of changing the singular to the plural is to add the letter -s, for example: classroom + s = classrooms

If the singular noun ends in -s, -x, -sh or -ch, you must add -es to form the plural, because without the help of the letter -e in -es, you would not be able to hear the sound of the final -s.

(b) Saying the plural of glass as 'glasss' and marsh as 'marshs' make very odd sounds, but adding -es instead, makes it possible to sing the old song:

'With a ladder and some glasses,
You could see to Hackney Marshes,
If it wasn't for the houses in between.'

(c) Write out the plural of the following words.

1 watch	8 inch	15 address
2 bench	9 patch	16 grass
3 bush	10 walrus	17 box
4 gas	11 church	18 fizz
5 fox	12 wish	19 pouch
6 buzz	13 witch	20 princess
7 kiss	14 tax	

(d) You have been given a list of items to buy at the greengrocer:

one cucumber
one lettuce
one box of chicory
one bunch of water-cress
one branch of celery
one batch of spring-onions
one bundle of radishes
one pound of tomatoes

Just as you are leaving, you are told to alter the list by putting 'two' instead of 'one' for each item. Write out the new list.

(e) Write out the following sentences, changing every singular noun to plural, and making the verbs plural.

1 The rabbit runs from the dog.
2 The girl wears a blue dress.
3 I keep the thrush in a cage.
4 The prince spoke to the princess.
5 There was a walrus in the pool.
6 The actress carries a suitcase.
7 The waitress served the customer.
8 The glass had a deep scratch.
9 The student sat on a bench.
10 The lioness was pacing the cage next to that of a fierce tigress.

Billy, in one of his nice new *sashes*,
Fell in the fire and was burnt to *ashes*;
Now, although the room goes chilly,
I haven't the heart to poke poor Billy.

THE PLURAL OF NOUNS ENDING IN 'F' OR 'FE'

I went to the baker and from a _____
He gave me two crusty _____.
I carefully cut each _____ in _____
And arranged them on two _____.

Don't ask me where I put those _____,
Just look for them your _____.

1 If the singular noun ends in _f, change it to _v before adding _es to form the plural, for example:

wolf — wolves
calf — calves   self — selves

Also, if the singular noun ends in _fe, the plural changes to _ves, for example:

wife — wives
life — lives   knife — knives

2 Words which end in double f (_ff) always end in _ffs, for example:

cliff — cliffs   cuff — cuffs
staff — staffs   puff — puffs

3 Write out the following, putting in the words **thief**, **leaf**, **leaves** and **belief** in the blank spaces.

I knew a _____, and to my relief,
He promised to turn over
A brand new _____.

It's my _____ though, to my sorrow,
That although he believes
In starting new_____,
Each day he will say,
'There's no harm in delay;
I will start a new _____ tomorrow.'

4 Write out the following, putting in the words **half**, **halves**, **leaf**, **loaves**, **shelf**, **shelves** and **selves** in the spaces, using each word once only.

5 There are a few words ending in _f which do not follow the _ves rule; the _f stays where it is and refuses to 'run away', for example:

proof — proofs
roof — roofs
reef — reefs
chief — chiefs
belief — beliefs
grief — griefs

6 The following words are unusual because they may be written either with _fs or _ves:

hoof — hoofs or hooves
scarf — scarfs or scarves
wharf — wharfs or wharves
dwarf — dwarfs or dwarves
handkerchief — handkerchiefs or handkerchieves

I know a hostess who likes to pour custard *herself* over the pudding before serving, but I prefer to let my guests pour it over *themselves*.

PLURAL OF NOUNS ENDING IN 'Y'

"GET RID OF THE Y"
CONSONANT +

> If a singular noun ends in –y, look at the letter before the –y; if it is a *consonant* change the –y to –ies in order to form the plural, for example:

BABY → BAB
BAB + IES = BABIES

> If the letter before the –y is a vowel, keep the –y and just add –s.

"SAVE THE Y"

TRAY + S = TRAYS

(a) Write out the plural of the following.

spy	key	lady
alley	story	storey
penny	ferry	jelly
abbey	puppy	lorry
library	journey	family
diary	dairy	essay
quay	melody	monkey
party	holiday	salary
enemy	convoy	territory
volley	birthday	monastery
turkey	quarry	allergy
jersey	display	fairy
berry	whisky	buoy
estuary	alloy	piggery

(b) Write out the following, putting these words in the blank spaces.

storeys	chimneys	flies
kidneys	trolleys	stories
strawberries	donkeys	

1 Mrs Jones bought a red fly-swatter. She wasted her money; she couldn't find red _____ anywhere.

2 What did the tall stack say to the two little _____!'
'You're too small to smoke!'

3 'There I was, on the top floor of a hotel of twenty _____ . . .'
'Is this going to be another one of your tall _____?'

4 'I've been promoted transport manager of the supermarket.'
'What do you do?'
'I look after the _____.'

5 'Doctor, I need something for my _____!'
'Certainly — here's some bacon.'

6 'What's the best way to raise _____?'
Use a spoon!'

7 'Tell me, how long can _____ live without brains?'
'How old are you?'

PLURAL OF NOUNS ENDING IN 'O'

ECHOES ECHOES ECHOES
ECHO
ECHO ECHO

> If a singular noun ends in the letter –o, look at the letter before the –o. If it is a consonant, add the letters –es.

ECHO + ES = ECHOES

(a) There are a few words which do not obey this rule, e.g.:

photo — photos   halo — halos
kilo — kilos   dynamo — dynamos

This also applies to some words connected with music, for example:
piano — pianos   solo — solos

> If the letter before the –o is a vowel, add the letter –s.

RADIO + S = RADIOS

(b) Write out the plural of the following words.

cargo	hero	studio
motto	Negro	curio
stereo	video	cameo
veto	potato	tomato
patio	rodeo	domino
cuckoo	kangaroo	cockatoo
volcano	tornado	torpedo
buffalo	commando	embargo
mosquito	stiletto	portfolio
Eskimo	innuendo	manifesto

UNUSUAL PLURALS

(a) There are a few words which do not make use of the –s but instead, form the plural by a change in spelling, for example:

woman (the a becomes e) — women
foot   — feet   tooth   — teeth
louse — lice   mouse — mice
goose — geese   child   — children
man   — men

(b) Note the plural for compound words:
brother-in-law — brothers-in-law
(you mean more than one brother, not more than one law)
spoonful and bucketful change to:
spoonfuls and bucketfuls (you mean more than one contents of the item, not more than one spoon or bucket)

> 'Come and play golf with us!
> Are you a man or a mouse?'
> 'I'm a man — my wife is scared of *mice*.'

NO, KNOW AND NOW

> NO: I've no idea
> KNOW: To know the answer
> NOW: Now is the time

SEEK TO KNOW

Write out the following, putting **no**, **know** or **now** inside the spaces.

1   'A thermos-flask keeps hot things hot and cold things cold.'
   'How does it _____?'
2   Hundreds of customers use our cleaning service. They _____ _____ better.
3   Inflation, you _____, has changed things. _____ one can live as cheaply as two used to.
4   What two people _____ may be a secret. What three people _____ is a secret _____ longer.
5   'Don't be afraid of Rover, little boy. You _____ the saying, "A barking dog never bites", don't you?'
   'I _____ it and you _____ it,' said the boy, 'but does the dog _____ it?'
6   'Mary, to what family does the walrus belong?'
   'I don't _____, Miss. _____ family in our street has one.'
7   '_____ look here, William — stop showing off. Do you think that you're the teacher here?'
   '—, Sir, I — I'm not.'
   'Then stop acting like a fool!'

> 'Did you *know* there's an idiot who goes around saying no?'
> '*No.*'
> 'Oh, it's you!'

NEW AND KNEW THREW AND THROUGH

> NEW: A brand new dress
> KNEW: They knew the answer
> THREW: He threw a stone
> THROUGH: To go through a door

(a)   Write out the following, putting **knew** or **new** in the spaces.

There were three boys, one of whom was a _____ boy; the other two were Albert and John, who had been at school for two years. When Albert and John arrived at school, the teacher said: 'This is _____ for you two, why are you so late?'
The boys replied, 'Sorry, sir, but we have been so occupied with throwing pebbles into the river, that we forgot the time.'
Just then, the _____ boy walked in, soaking wet, and in a pool of water, stood in front of the teacher's desk.
'Ah, the _____ boy,' said the teacher.
'I _____ you were coming today. What's your name?'
'Pebbles, sir.'

(b)   Write out the following, putting **threw** or **through** in the spaces.
1   Walk _____ our antique shop and buy what your grandmother _____ away.
2   'It was _____ you I got this black eye. I tried out your joke of pretending to forget my wife's wedding anniversary, and she _____ the soup at me.'
   'But it wouldn't give you a black eye if she _____ the soup at you!'
   'It did. It was still in the tin!'

WHO'S AND WHOSE

> 'I say, who's that being thrown out of "WHO'S WHO"?'
> 'I'm not sure; it's a chap whose face is familiar, but whose name I can't remember.'

WHO'S (stands for 'who is')
This is Mary who's coming with us. (This is Mary who is coming with us.)

WHOSE (stands for ownership)
This is my friend to whose house we have been invited.
(You could not use 'who's' in the above sentence because it would be the same as: 'This is my friend to who is house we have been invited.')

(b) Write out the following, putting 'whose' or 'who's' in the spaces.

1 'I am his Highness' dog at Kew;
   Pray tell me, sir, _____ dog are you?'
2 The pig _____ house was built of bricks, sang: '_____ afraid of the big bad Wolf?'
3 Two cannibals fighting, raises the question,
   _____ tough hide will give indigestion?
   They've lighted their fires and made water hot;
   I wonder just who will end up in _____ pot!

Special note: Who's can also mean who has.
'Who's finished his *exercise*?'
('Who has finished his *exercise*?')

YOUR AND YOU'RE

Do you see where I am replaced by an apostrophe? After the 'u' — NOT after the 'r'.

(a) 'You're next!' equals 'You are next!'

'Go and get your jacket!' does not mean 'Go and get you are jacket!' It means the jacket that belongs to you.

(b) Write out the following, putting **'you're'** or **'your'** in the spaces.

1 If all the cars are coming your way,
   _____ going the wrong way in a one-way street.
2 _____ attention, please! This is a staff announcement for Driver Jones. '_____ taking out the wrong train!'
3 'I don't care if _____ Santa Claus, get _____ reindeer off my roof!'
4 '_____ old, Father William,' the young man said,
   'And _____ hair has become very white;
   And yet _____ incessantly propped on _____ head.
   Do you think, at _____ age, it is right?'
   With apologies to Edward Lear

> 'Why is *your* dog glaring at me like that?'
> '*You're* eating from his dish.'

THERE, THEIR AND THEY'RE

place:
standing over there

possessive:
their brushes and
paints

abbreviation:
meaning 'they are'

Write out the following, putting 'their',
'there' or 'they're' in the spaces.

1 'As I was going up the stair
   I met a man who wasn't _____.
   He wasn't _____ again today,
   I wish, I wish he'd stay away.'
2 The horses are lined up at the starting-
   gate! _____ off!
3 '. . . so that men will still say, ''This was
   _____ finest hour.'''
4 'Oh, to be in England,
   Now that April's _____ . . .'
   Not for me. I say let them keep _____
   April. I will spend April in Spain where
   _____ more friendly, and _____
   weather isn't always wind and rain.

> 'I'm not afraid to die. I just don't want
> to be *there* when it happens.'

THEIRS AND THERE'S

Write out the following, putting 'there's' or
'theirs' in the spaces.

1 'If you can keep your head when all
   about you are losing _____ . . .'
   you will be the only one with a head!
2 '_____ an old mill by the stream, where
   we used to sit and dream.'
3 '_____ not to reason why,
   _____ but to do and die:
   Into the valley of Death
   Rode the six hundred.'
4 '_____ no business like show-business,
   it's one business we know.
   Actors, singers, dancers, _____ is the
   life; I don't think _____ anything more
   exciting.'
5 'If so be, you ask me where
   They do grow? I answer, there,
   Where my Julia's lips do smile;
   _____ the land, of cherry-isle.'
6 '_____ got to be an easier way of
   making-money than this!'
   'Well, _____ always counterfeiting!'

Note: **There's** may also be used in place
of 'there has', for example:
'I hear there's been an accident.'
('I hear there has been an accident.')

HERE AND HERE'S, HEAR AND HEARS

WHERE, WEAR, WERE AND WE'RE

abbreviation:
short for 'here is'

place: right here

verb: I can hear you

he hears
me speak

abbreviation:
short for 'we are'

verb: we were there

place: where are you?

verb: to wear your clothes

(a) Write out the following, putting 'here', 'hear' or 'here's' in the spaces.

1 _____ a good place to sit.
We won't be able to _____ that awful singer from _____.
2 '_____ of a Sunday morning
My love and I would lie,
And see the coloured counties,
And _____ the larks so high
About us in the sky.'
3 Faith, Sir, _____ our chance, for we are _____ today, and gone tomorrow.
4 'Waiter, did I _____ that you serve crabs _____?'
'We serve anyone. Sit down, sir. _____ the menu.'

Write out the following, putting 'wear', 'were', 'where' or 'we're' in the spaces.

1 _____ on earth did you pick up that dreadful expression 'we was'? You should always say 'we _____'!
2 Oh, dear, _____ lost, Mary! Take out the map and let's see _____ we are, and whether we _____ driving on the right road. This outing is going to _____ me out!
3 Home is the place _____, whatever you _____ and even if you go about in rags and don't _____ decent clothes, when you have to go there, they have to take you in and say '_____ glad you're back!'

OFF AND OF

> **If it sounds like 'ov' you spell it 'of'; if it concerns movement you spell it 'off'.**

(a) Write out the following, putting 'of' or 'off' in the spaces.

1 Don't let worry kill you _____, let the Church help.
2 'John, where were you yesterday?'
   'I went _____ for a haircut, sir.'
   'What! In school time?'
   'But sir, it grew in school time.'
   'Not all _____ it.'
   'But I didn't have all _____ it _____, sir.'
3 'Don't be afraid, little boy. This dog will eat _____ your hand.'
   'That's what I'm afraid _____!'
4 Notice in the window _____ a second-hand shop:
   'Mrs Smith has cast-_____ clothing_____ every description.'

> **'I've just discovered my boyfriend has a wooden leg — should I break it *off*?'**

TO, TOO AND TWO

(b) TO   means towards something.
TWO means the figure 2.
TOO has an extra 'o' with an 'eye' to see if something is too big or too small. In addition, it can be used to mean 'also'.

Write out the following, putting 'to', 'too' or 'two' in the spaces.

1 You have _____ points and John has twenty _____; how many do you need to be equal?
   Answer: You need twenty _____.
2 I'm in a tender mood today
   And feel poetic _____;
   For fun I'll just dash off _____ lines
   And send them off _____ you.
3 It takes _____ _____ speak the truth — one _____ speak and one _____ hear.
4 What did the male owl tell the female owl in the pouring rain?
   'It's _____ wet _____ woo.'
5 There are _____ kinds of people at parties — those who want _____ go home and those who want _____ be the last _____ leave. The trouble is that they are usually married _____ each other.
6 Inflation means that _____ people can now live as cheaply as _____ used _____.

> **'What's the difference between a hungry boy and a greedy boy?'**
> **'One longs *to* eat and the other eats *too* long.'**

FOR, FORE AND FOUR

FOR — as in 'go for a walk'
FORE — as in 'the front part of a ship'
FOUR — as in 'one, two, three, four'

FOUR IS A NUMBER

(a) Write out the following, putting **for**, **fore** or **four** in the spaces.

1 'This new aid _____ hearing is so small that nobody notices it.'
   'What kind is it?'
   'Half-past _____.'

2 'Are you the _____ man in charge?'
   'Oh no, sir. Mike over there is the _____ man; I'm the number one man.'

3 _____ men of the jury asked Mr Smith if he would act as _____ man of the jury.

4 'Doctor, _____ teen days ago I made a decision to come and see you, and now I'm here. Doctor, I think I'm schizophrenic!'
   'Thank you _____ coming. Please sit down, and the _____ of us can discuss our problem.'

5 Some people make excuses _____ what a man has said when drunk, but I think that what is said when drunk, has really been thought out be_hand.

6 'Dame _tune smile, and make me win.
   _ty _'s what I want to win.
   The croupier gives the wheel a spin;
   _ty three! See the croupier grin!'

7 'What goes "moo moo" and "oom oom"?'
   'A cow walking _____ and backward.'

8 At a _____ some golf match between two pairs of players, the first man started off with a roar of '_____!'

Newsboy: 'Forty-four people swindled!
         Forty-four people swindled!'
Passer-by: 'I'll buy a paper. Hey!
           This is yesterday's!'
Newsboy: 'Forty-five people swindled!
         Forty-five people swindled!'

9 _____ _____ty pence you can buy, _____ and twenty blackbirds baked in a pie.

10 'Was none who would be _most
   To lead such a dire attack;
   But those behind cried "_ward!'
   And those be_ cried "Back!"'

(b) Write out the following, putting these words in the spaces:

–going   –noon   –ground
–seen   –cast   –warning

'Here is the weather fore_. In the fore_ the details clearly show the clouds bringing the rain, of which we had no fore_. In the next twenty-four hours, the clouds will disperse and the fore_ will be sunny, although more rain is fore_ in the afternoon.
All the fore_ has come by satellite.'

Scribbled on a wall:
'I'm an anakist — I wanna be free!'
Written neatly below:
'I want to be *four* and be able to spell.'

PAST AND PASSED

PASSED IS A VERB
PAST IS NOT A VERB

The word **passed** may be used in one way only, as an action word.
'. . . as he passed.' (verb)

The word **past** may be used in many ways, but not as a verb.
'. . . as he flashed past.'
The word 'flashed' is the verb.

Write out the following, putting 'passed' or 'past' in the spaces.

1 'What's your son going to be when he has _____ his A-levels?'
  'An old-age pensioner.'
2 'What's the time?'
  'It is half _____ two, and time you bought yourself a watch.'
3 People say: 'In times _____ things were better; the present is worse than the
  _____.'
  I have _____ this way of thinking, but I know that those who cannot remember the _____ are condemned to repeat the mistakes of times that have _____ by.

'Mummy, Daddy just fell off the roof!'
'I know, dear; I saw him as he *passed*.'

WHETHER AND WEATHER

'I don't know whether to say yes or no.'

RAINY WEATHER

Whether gives a doubt or a choice between alternatives.

Weather is hot or cold, wet or dry.

Write out the following, putting 'whether' or 'weather' in the spaces.

1 Special Offer! Snow shovels reduced from £5 to £3 owing to lack of bad _____.
2 'Young man, I don't know _____ you deserve being helped out of that tree. Fancy coming down in a parachute in this foggy _____!'
  'Lady, I was *not* coming down. My foot got caught in the _____ balloon, and I was going *up*!'
3 'The staff of the Met. Office are on strike, so I do not know _____ we shall be able to give you a _____ forecast tonight, but there will definitely be no _____ tomorrow.'

'Brethren,' declared the Parson, winding up his sermon on the subject of prudence, 'we must each decide *whether* to be in the light with the wise Virgins or in the dark with the foolish ones.'

WRITE AND RIGHT

'**Right, my lad! You have the right to remain silent, but I will write down anything you say, and it may be used as evidence.**'

RIGHT TURN!

Write out the following, putting 'write' or 'right' in the spaces.

1 'Squad! By the _____, turn! Quick march! Left, _____, left, _____.'
2 'Now you are married, I think you have done the _____ thing to _____ your will.'
3 'If you wish to _____ the story of my success, it is being in the _____ place at the _____ time. By the way, my watch has stopped: What *is* the _____ time?'
4 'I have to _____ out fifty times: "It is not _____ to _____ the word _____ without the letter W."''
5 'Which is the _____ hand to _____ with?'
'Neither. You _____ with a pen.'

'**I would give my *right* hand to be able to *write* ambidextrously.**'

QUIET AND QUITE ALOUD AND ALLOWED

QUITE IS
COMPLETE
ALL ARE
ALLOWED
YOU SHOUT
ALOUD!

QUITE means 'completely, entirely, to the utmost extent'.
QUITE can also mean 'somewhat, to some extent', for example:

The bus took quite a long time to arrive. She bought quite a few Christmas presents. ('She bought a considerable number of Christmas presents.')

Write out the following, putting **quiet**, **quite**, **aloud** or **allowed** in the spaces.

1 *Teacher:* 'Everybody keep _____, please. What three words are most used in this classroom?'
Pupils (together): 'We don't know!'
Teacher: ' _____ correct!'
2 *Park-keeper:* 'Hey, you! Can't you read the notice: "Swimming in this lake is not _____."?'
'I'm not swimming . . . I'm drowning!'
Keeper: 'Oh, that's all right then.'
3 'Boy! You can't sleep in my class!'
'But, Sir, if you would talk in a _____ voice, I would be able to sleep _____ easily.'
4 'It's very _____ captain, too _____. I don't like it!'
'Go to sleep, soldier; everything is going to be _____ all right. I can assure you that when everything is nice and _____, it means that we are _____ safe from the en . . .'

THE PREFIX

BEFORE   AFTER

RE + JOINED → REJOINED

> **The prefix is a group of letters placed at the beginning of a word in order to change or extend its meaning.**

It sometimes happens that a word with a prefix has nothing to do with the same word without a prefix.

'That musician friend of yours — is he still **composing**?'
'No, he died last year. Right now, he's **decomposing**!'

(a) A few prefixes do not join on to words but are joined with a hyphen, for example:

non- (meaning 'not')
non-smoking compartment

co- (meaning 'together', 'jointly')
co-operative
Note: No hyphen is wanted if the word begins with an 'e', as in 'coeducation'.

counter- (meaning 'against')
counter-cheering

ex- (meaning 'formerly', 'once been')
ex-serviceman

vice- ('in place of', 'next in rank')
vice-captain

(b) Write out the following words putting one of the above prefixes in front, as appropriate (some may have two prefixes).

attack	directory	existence
clockwise	attendance	author
enemy	admiral	equal
intelligence	revolution	warden

(c) The following prefixes are sometimes spelled incorrectly.

bi (meaning 'doubly', 'twice')
bi + cycle = bicycle
(think of 'bi' as part of 'bikes')

poly (meaning 'many', 'much')
poly + gon = polygon
(only one 'l', because a 'polly gone' is a dead parrot)

fore (meaning 'in front', 'beforehand')
fore + arm = forearm

anti (meaning 'against', 'opposite')
anti + septic = antiseptic

ante (meaning 'before', 'preceding')
ante + natal = antenatal

ANTI =   **ANTE =**
AGAINST   **BEFORE**

(d) Write out the following, putting one of the above prefixes in front.

1	vivisection	9	technic	17	court
2	penultimate	10	ennial	18	fathers
3	diluvian	11	lingual	19	shorten
4	syllabic	12	climax	20	biotic
5	nuptial	13	social	21	theism
6	closure	14	annual	22	freeze
7	monthly	15	gamy	23	cast
8	chamber	16	cyclone	24	glot

> *Vicar (baptizing a baby):*   **'What is the name of your child, Mrs Unsaturates?'**
> 'Polly.'
> **'I name this child Polly Unsaturates.'**

THE PREFIX

ONE WAY STREET

PREFIX → WORD

> To give the opposite meaning to a word, there is a choice of several different prefixes.

(a) A prefix can give a word an opposite meaning, for example:

happy with the prefix un = unhappy

If the word begins with the letter 'n', you must not lose the 'n' of the prefix 'un'.

necessary + un = unnecessary

In addition to 'un', the following also have the meaning of 'not': im in il ir

(b) The problem of the word 'possible':
To say 'unpossible', sounds wrong, and 'inpossible' is hard to say.
The answer is — impossible.

Use the prefix 'im' before 'p':
polite + im = impolite

Use the prefix 'im' before 'm':
material + im = immaterial

Make sure that you do not lose the 'm' from the prefix 'im'; note that there are two letters 'm' in the word 'immaterial'.

(c) To use the prefix 'in' with a word beginning with the letter 'l' is awkward (try saying 'inlegal'). Instead, use the prefix 'il', but make certain that you do not lose the 'l' from the prefix 'il', for example:

legal + il = illegal

(d) It is too awkward to say 'inrational', so before a word beginning with the letter 'r', the prefix is changed to 'ir'. Make certain that you do not lose the 'r' from the prefix 'ir', for example:

rational + ir = irrational

(e) Write out the following, and by means of a prefix, give the opposite meanings to the words printed in italics.

1 'There is no such thing as a moral or an *moral* book. Books are well written, or badly written.'
2 Man can believe in the *possible* but not in the *probable*.
3 'To my mind, there is nothing so *liberal* and so ill-bred as loud laughter.'
4 'Murder, most foul as in the best it is; But this most foul, strange and *natural*.'
5 'I have caught an everlasting cold; I have lost my voice most *recoverably*.'
6 'The moan of doves in *memorial* elms, And murmuring of *numerable* bees.'

(f) The prefix 'dis' means 'not', but can also mean 'apart or away'. When using it before a word beginning with 's', make sure you do not lose the letter 's' from 'dis', for example:

satisfaction + dis = dissatisfaction

Write out the following words, putting 'dis' in front, and be careful to use one 's' or double 's', as required.

similar	appoint	service
appear	sociate	approve
simulate	agree	soluble
qualify	solve	pleasure

> 'Is your dog a setter or a pointer?'
> 'Neither — he's an UPsetter and a DISappointer.'

THE SUFFIX

The suffixes 'ed' and 'ing' are dealt with on page 2, and the problem of the letter 'e' when adding a suffix, is dealt with on page 4. Similarly, the problem of the letter 'y' appears on pages 5 and 8. On pages 10 and 11 will be found the subject of the consonant before a suffix is added, and on pages 14 and 15 are the special problems of the letters 'r' and 'l'.

FLY AND 'ER'
CLING TOGETHER TO MAKE A NEW WORD — 'FLYER'

> The suffix is a letter or a group of letters, added to a word to change the meaning of the word or way the word is used — play + er = player.

(a) The suffix 'ly' is used to turn a describing word like 'swift' (the cheetah is a **swift** animal) into an adverb 'swiftly' (the cheetah runs more **swiftly** than a deer).

If you refer to page 4, you will note that if a word ending with 'e' has 'ly' added, the 'e' stays with the word, for example:

love + ly = lovely

Page 8 explains that if 'ly' is added to a word ending in 'y', the 'y' must be changed to an 'i', for example:

happy + ly = happily

An actor is not **necessarily** conceited: he just likes to admire himself **objectively**.

(b) Take care that if you add 'ly' to a word ending in 'l', the 'l' is not lost, for example:

annual + ly = annually
('annually' contains **two** letter 'l')

(c) Write out the following, putting the following ten words in the spaces.

1 reflectively	5 defensively	8 fully
2 especially	6 really	9 usually
3 leisurely	7 finally	10 wholly
4 gradually		

1 The black cats gr_ eased under the gate, like dark treacle, and fin_ melted away in the darkness.
2 Sleep and health are not f_ and w_ enjoyed until after they have been interrupted.
3 It is r_ hard to give away kindness, e_ to country folk — it is u_ returned.
4 An elephant and a mouse were walking l_ through the jungle.
  The elephant said r_: 'You are very small, you know.'
  'Well,' said the mouse d_,
  'I've been very ill.'

(d) Add 'ly' to the following words.

1 mental	5 fatal	9 local
2 equal	6 mortal	10 actual
3 royal	7 manual	11 total
4 rascal	8 initial	12 comical

THE SUFFIX

'I say, Holmes, how do you spell
"elementary"?'
E-L-E-M-E-N-T-A-R-Y, my dear Watson!'

(a)   The suffixes 'ery', 'ary', and 'ory':

The suffix 'ery' is added to a 'root' word which is able to stand on its own without the suffix, for example:

You may *slip* if it is slip*ery*.
A *nurse* is employed in a nurs*ery*.

The suffixes 'ary' and 'ory' are usually a part of the 'root' word and do not make *sense* without the suffix, for example:

libr*ary*   laborat*ory*

There is no such thing as a 'libr', neither is there such a thing as a 'laborat'; the suffixes 'ary' and 'ory' are an essential part of these words.

(b)   Write out the following, putting the letter 'e', 'a' or 'o' in the spaces.

Janu_ry	access_ry	invent_ry
ordin_ry	introduct_ry	milit_ry
prelimin_ry	flatt_ry	necess_ry
jewell_ry	contr_ry	compuls_ry
discov_ry	secret_ry	transit_ry
explanat_ry	vocabul_ry	predat_ry
Febru_ry	machin_ry	

Note these exceptions to the rule:

surgery	stationery	embroidery
cemetery	monastery	mystery

(c)   The suffixes 'ful' and 'fully':

'Tuesday's child is *full* of grace.'
(Tuesday's child is grace*ful*.)

When used as a suffix, 'full' loses an 'l' and is written as 'ful'.

If you need to add '*ly*' to '*ful*', you must double the 'l', so that the suffix is written '*fully*'.

Tuesday's child acts **gracefully**.

(d)   Write out the following words, adding the suffixes 'ful' and 'fully' to each one, for example:

beauty   beauti*ful*   beauti*fully*

1	peace	4	truth	7	mercy
2	play	5	pain	8	shame
3	pity	6	faith	9	use

(e)   Note the following special cases:

skill	skilful	skilfully
will	wilful	wilfully
fill	fulfil	fulfilment

(f)   The suffixes 'less' and 'ness':

Do not leave out the last letter of the root word if it happens to be the same as the first letter of the suffix, for example:

soul   + less = soulless
sudden + ness = suddenness

Write out the following, putting one of these words in the spaces.

1	cleanness	3 goalless
2	drunkenness	4 keenness

Although the football match ended in a _____ draw, we appreciated the _____ of the players, the _____ of the game, and the absence of _____ on the terraces.

'Be a *missionary*! Give cannibals a taste of Christianity!'

THE SUFFIX

(a) The suffixes 'able' and 'ible':

The suffix 'able' is used after 'root' words that are complete by themselves, or almost complete, for example:

use + able = usable   (take off the 'e' from 'use' as shown on page 3)
usable means *able* to be used

eat + able = eatable   (*able* to be eaten)

(b) The suffix 'ible' is used after a part of a word which cannot stand by itself.

audible means something that can be heard (it is possible to be heard, but you are not able to 'aud' something)

eligible (you are not able to 'elig')
defensible means 'easily defended', but as you are not able to 'easily defended', the suffix 'ible' is used

(c) When to use the suffix 'able':
1 After a root word as shown above.
2 After the letter 'i' — sociable.
3 After a hard 'c' or a hard 'g':
   edu<u>c</u>ate + able = educable
   navi<u>g</u>ate + able = navigable

US**ABLE**
ABLE TO BE USED
AUD**IBLE**
POSS**IBLE** TO BE HEARD

(d) Write out the following, putting 'a' or 'i' in the spaces.

believ_ble	reli_ble	sens_ble
irrit_ble	forc_ble	attain_ble
accept_ble	digest_ble	admir_ble
permiss_ble	convert_ble	vis_ble
respect_ble	neglig_ble	indel_ble
practic_ble	service_ble	leg_ble

(e) Note the following exceptions in the use of the suffixes 'able' and 'ible':

inevitable	probable	portable
formidable	indomitable	memorable
flexible	collapsible	resistible

'Do you have any *invisible* ink?'
'Certainly, sir. What colour?'

(f)   The suffixes –'ise' and –'ize':

For words in which both endings are acceptable, use 'ize' rather than 'ise'. For example, one may write 'realize' or 'realise', but *realize* is preferable. However, there are many words in which the spelling of the suffix *must* be 'ise', as in the following:

advertise	advise	compromise
despise	devise	disguise
enterprise	exercise	expertise
improvise	incise	merchandise
precise	revise	supervise
surmise	surprise	televise

(g)   The suffixes 'ceed' and 'cede':

This is easily remembered because there are only three words which end in 'ceed', e.g.:

exceed   proceed   succeed

all the rest use the ending 'cede':

concede	precede	recede
secede	accede	intercede
etc.		

'What always *succeeds*?'
'A canary with no teeth.'

THE SUFFIX

(a) The suffixes 'ent', 'ence', 'ant' and 'ance'.

'Ent' and 'ence' are much more usual than 'ant' and 'ance'.

In most cases, if the suffix has the meaning of 'a person who . . .' or 'something to do with . . .', use 'ant', for example:

assist + ant = assistant
(a person who . . . gives help to others)
import + ant = important
(something to do with . . . a matter of great consequence)

The suffix 'ance' is often used to mean 'to do with a state of . . .', for example:

disturb + ance = disturbance
(to do with a state of . . . having rest and quiet interrupted)

(b) In many cases, if the suffix has the meaning of 'a quality of being . . .', we use the suffixes 'ent' and 'ence', for example:

excellent	(a quality of being . . . surpassingly good)
efficient	(a quality of being . . . competent and capable)
convenience	(a quality of being . . . suitable and agreeable)

(c) Write out the following, adding the suffixes 'ence' and 'ance'.

1 assist_	5 exist_	9 confid_
2 intellig_	6 disappear_	10 consequ_
3 experi_	7 circumst_	11 insur_
4 obedi_	8 signific_	12 resembl_

The Scrabble board:

DOUBLE WORD SCORE			DOUBLE LETTER SCORE			DOUBLE WORD SCORE		
	DOUBLE WORD SCORE		C_3			DOUBLE WORD SCORE		
		TRIPLE LETTER SCORE	A_1		TRIPLE LETTER SCORE			
			DOUBLE LETTER SCORE / R_1	DOUBLE LETTER SCORE / A_1			DOUBLE LETTER SCORE	
DOUBLE LETTER SCORE	C_3	A_1	R_1	E_1	L_1	E_1	S_1	S_1
			DOUBLE LETTER SCORE / F_4	DOUBLE LETTER SCORE			DOUBLE LETTER SCORE	
		TRIPLE LETTER SCORE	U_1		TRIPLE LETTER SCORE			
	DOUBLE LETTER SCORE		L_1			DOUBLE LETTER SCORE		
DOUBLE WORD SCORE			DOUBLE LETTER SCORE			DOUBLE WORD SCORE		

(d) Write out the following, putting in the suffixes in the blank spaces.

1 'Do you think the world's troubles are due to apathy or to ignor_?'
'I don't know, and I don't care.'

2 A man went to a psychiat_ complain_ of an inferior_ complex.
After many visits, he was told:
'Sir, you don't have a complex.
You really are inferior!'

3 A reason_ amount of fleas is good for a dog; it keeps him from introspec_, and brood_ over being a dog.

4 'Object_, your Honour! My learned friend is trying to draw a conclu_ from the prosecu_ witness.'
Judge: 'May I see that? It doesn't look like a conclu_ to me. Can't you draw any better than that?'

5 'Live your own life, I say. Take my uncle. He's never had a day of activ_ in his life, smokes all day and drinks all night. He's as happy and healthy a man as anyone else in the inten_ care ward.'

Voice from loudspeaker: 'We have to report with *reluctance* that there are no toilets on the rear part of the train. We apologize for the *inconvenience*.'

King, speaking to the Queen:
'What do you mean, let's start calling it a *queendom*?'

54

'DISAPPEARING' LETTERS

**The 'e' and 'i', no longer staying,
Are disappearing without paying!**

> **Most words do not change when a suffix is added, but there are some in which a letter is left out — particularly 'u', 'e' and 'i'.**

(a) In the case of many words ending in 'our' or 'ous' to which a suffix is added, the letter 'u' has to 'get up and disappear', for example:

humour (add the suffix 'ous')
humo*r — humor + ous — hum<u>o</u>rous
humo*r — humor + ist — hum<u>o</u>rist

curious (add the suffix 'ity')
curio*s — curios + ity — curi<u>o</u>sity

(b) Examples of the disappearing 'i':

vain — va*n + ity — v<u>a</u>nity
exclaim — excla*m — excl<u>a</u>mation
explain — expla*n — expl<u>a</u>nation

(c) The letter 'e' sometimes has to disappear when it is followed by an 'r' and a suffix is added. Here are some words where the suffix 'ess' is used to show the female gender:

tiger — tig*r + ess — tigress
waiter — wait*r + ess — waitress
enchanter — enchant*r — enchantress

Other examples of the 'e' being dropped from the word ending 'er':

winter — wint*r + y — win<u>tr</u>y
monster — monst*r + ous — mon<u>str</u>ous
hinder — hind*r + ance — hin<u>dr</u>ance
register — regist*r + ar — regi<u>str</u>ar
administer — administ*r — admini<u>str</u>ate

(d) Note the following words in which more than one letter has to disappear:

pronounce — pron<u>unc</u>iation
maintain — main<u>ten</u>ance
humble — hum<u>ili</u>ty

(e) Write out the following words, providing an appropriate suffix, for example: enter — entrance.

1 glamour	11 carpenter
2 repeat	12 cylinder
3 proclaim	13 vapour
4 emperor	14 disaster
5 wonder	15 remember
6 labour	16 generous
7 repeat	17 impetuous
8 generous	18 vigorous
9 monster	19 favour
10 valour	20 honour

(f) Write out the following, putting in the missing letters.

1 This plaque is in memory of the members of the choir who died singing as cho_ in this church.
2 We are gripped with terror at the idea of being terr_.
3 The cost of having to maintain the churchyard has risen, and in future, parishioners will have to take care of the maint_ round their own graves.

> *Notice:* Found: false teeth in the car park of the 'Daily Echo'. Please come in and smile at the *receptionist,* and she will return them to you.

CHANGING FIGURES TO WORDS

'SEVEN, EIGHT, NINE, SEVEN, NINE ... OR IS IT SIX?'

> Amounts of money, dates, and large numbers, are written down in figures. In other cases, it is more usual to write figures down in words.

Spelling points to notice:

There is an 'e' in nine, nineteen, nineteenth and ninety, but not in ninth.

There is a 'u' in four, fourth, fourteen and fourteenth, but not in forty and fortieth.

There is a 'v' in five and twelve, but not in fifth, fifteen, fifty and twelfth.

When numbers end in 'y' (for example, seventy; change the 'y' to 'i' when you need to write 'seventies' or 'seventieth'.

To add units to twenty, use a hyphen (twenty plus five is twenty-five). This applies up to ninety-nine but not beyond. For example, in 'one hundred and ten', no hyphens are used.

Fractions also require a hyphen:
two-thirds   eleven-sixteenths

Write out the following, putting words in place of the figures.

1 'Hello, little boy, how old are you?'
'I am 7, sir.'
'And what are you going to be, my little man?'
'8, sir.'

2 'Which is correct? 9 and 5 **are** 13, or 9 and 5 **is** 13?'
'Neither: The answer is 14.'

3 My uncle was run over by a steam-roller. He is now in hospital, in rooms 33 to 36.

4 'What did they do when the Forth Bridge collapsed?'
'Built a 5th.'

5 When my dad was 22, he was a 7 stone weakling: now, at the age of 44, he's a 14 stone weakling.

6 My brother didn't know that $^8/_{10}$ths was the same as $^4/_5$ths until Dad bought him a pocket-calculator.

7 'Sir, you said we needed 40 runs to win and that if we scored 24 both wickets, we would do it. But, Sir, twice 24 is 48!'
'Wrong as usual, boy. I said we wanted 20 for both wickets.'

8 A minister told his congregation that there are 101 different sins.
He has already had 57 requests for the list.

9 'Sing a song of 6p, a pocket full of rye, 24 blackbirds baked in a pie.'

> After his *third* glass of brandy, the young officer declined a *fourth*.
> Pointing to the centre of the table, the Colonel said: 'You see those *eight* candles, my boy? Well, when they appear to be *sixteen*, you've had enough!'
> 'But, Sir,' the officer said, 'there are only *four* candles!'

'S' FOR A VERB: 'C' FOR A NOUN

(a) The following words are spelt with an 's' when they are verbs (action words) and with a 'c' when they are nouns.

VERBS	NOUNS
practise	practice
license	licence
prophesy	prophecy
devise	device
advise	advice

Your local doctor is called a 'G.P.' (General Practitioner). He is known as a G.P. because he has a place in your area which is his practice (noun) in which he will practise (verb) general medicine.

ADVISE IS A VERB

Example:
The girls do netball practice (noun) on "Wednesdays. They practise (verb) in the school gymnasium.

(b) Write out the following, putting the words prophecy, prophesy, practice, practise, licence, license, device, devise, advice or advise in the spaces.

1 An inventor has been able to _____ a way of eating micro-chips — he has invented a micro-fork.
2 If you can tell the difference between good and bad _____, you do not need anybody to _____ you.
3 Secretary on telephone:
'Our automatic answering _____ is away for repairs. This is a person speaking.'
4 'Everything gets easier in time, if only you _____.'
'How about getting up in the morning?'

5 'Good morning! I would like to take out a dog _____, please.'
'Certainly, sir. What name?'
'Rover.'
'Right, sir, when can Rover come in and pay the fee to _____ a dog?'
6 Every man has to _____ his own future and inherit his own past.
7 A practical man is a man who is able to _____ the mistakes of his ancestors.
8 Although we may admire the wisdom of people who come to us to be _____d, _____ is worth what it costs — nothing.
9 *Game Warden:* 'Stop! You're hunting with last year's _____.'
Hunter: 'Yes, but I'm only shooting at the ones I missed last year!'
10 You are not allowed to charge for legal a_____ without having a l_____ which entitles you to p_____ law and set up your own legal p_____.
11 'As a crystal-gazer, I make it my _____ always to _____ after the event has happened; it's too easy to be wrong if you make a _____ beforehand.'

Motorist: 'I would like you to *advise* me about changing the oil in my car.'
Mechanic: 'My *advice* is that you keep the oil and change the car.'

CAPITAL LETTERS

Capital letters are used for all proper nouns.
All names and words in titles have capitals.
Places, days and months have capitals.
I is a capital letter when used by itself.
Talking must begin with a capital letter.
Addresses on envelopes have capital letters.
Letters beginning paragraphs have capitals.
Sentences *always* begin with a capital letter.

'Hello, son, what's your name?'
'Small "i", sir.'
'And what are you going to be when you grow up?'
'A capital "I", sir.'

Write out the following, putting in all the capital letters needed.

1 A visiting american was staying at a surrey hotel and was asked whether he wanted english or continental breakfast. 'i want a good old-fashioned english breakfast,' he said.
When he had finished, he called the waiter. 'that was a grand meal. i suppose all the food was grown here.'
'oh, no, sir,' said the waiter, 'you had irish bacon, french eggs, italian tomatoes, danish crispbread, hungarian marmalade and new zealand butter.'

2 A turk went back to turkey after much travelling on english trains. 'they are the best in the world,' he said, 'with compartments for everybody. i have seen carriages not only labelled smoking, but also reading, bath and sandwich!'

3 An actor was offered £500 a week to work on a new film.
'that's good pay,' he said. 'what's it called?'
'*treasure island*,' replied the director. 'you will play long john silver. be on the set first thing on tuesday morning.'
'for that money,' said the actor, 'i don't mind starting monday.'
'not monday. on monday you're having your leg off.'

4 I was at an audition at the lyceum theatre where there was a woman singing on the stage. her voice was so awful that i turned to the man sitting beside me and remarked upon it. he replied very frostily: 'that is my wife.' pink with confusion, i hastily stammered, 'i didn't mean her voice was awful, only the song she was singing.' 'i wrote the song,' he said.

5 a small indian boy came to newtown mixed infants' school.
'ah, the new boy,' said miss jones, 'what is your name?'
'vankarataam narasimha.'
'how do you spell it?'
'my mother helps me.'

6 Explain the difference in meaning between the two ways the following radio news item has been written.

(a) '. . . and that is the end of The World News.'
(b) '. . . and that is the End of the World news.'

Doctor: 'You have, I am afraid, just one month to live.'
Patient: 'My God! Just thirty days!'
Doctor: 'Not quite, I'm afraid. Today is the first of *February*.'

WORDS FROM LATIN AND GREEK

> **The English language owes a great deal for its formation to ancient Latin and Greek.**

(a) Perhaps the best known example is centum — one hundred.
A centurion was an officer in command of a unit of a hundred soldiers in the ancient Roman army.

The word has since been made use of in many ways, for example:
cent — a hundredth of a US dollar
century — a period of a hundred years or a hundred runs at cricket
centigrade — having a hundred degrees
centimetre — one hundredth of a metre

(b) The following are eight Greek roots:

grapho — I write   chronos — time
tele — far   auto — self
logos — study   thermo — heat
phone — sound   micros — small

The following are eight words in which the above roots are used; match the English word with the appropriate root.

For example: grapho — tele*graph*

1 microphone   5 chronological
2 geology   6 paragraph
3 telephone   7 thermometer
4 microscope   8 autograph

(c) There are some words borrowed from Latin and Greek which keep their original form when used in the plural, for example:

memorand*um*   memorand*a* (plural)

Write out the following, matching the *plural word* given in the first column with its *singular form* given in the second column.

1 axes   stratum
2 bases   criterion
3 oases   nucleus
4 theses   larva
5 cacti   oasis
6 fungi   fungus
7 radii   phenomenon
8 termini   basis
9 nuclei   datum
10 data   radius
11 strata   thesis
12 criteria   axis
13 phenomena cactus
14 larvae   terminus

(d) The following are ten Latin roots:

bene — good   spectare — to look
audio — I hear   fractus — break
magnus — great   annus — year
aqua — water   scribo — I write
moveo — I move   signum — sign

Match the following ten English words with the appropriate Latin root.

1 spectator   6 magnificent
2 moveable   7 audience
3 anniversary   8 aquarium
4 beneficial   9 fracture
5 signature   10 scripture

> 'I'm glad I wasn't born in Athens.'
> 'Why's that?'
> 'I can't speak Greek!'

DIFFICULT WORDS

The following words are often mis-spelt; the letters underlined are where the mistakes generally occur.

accessible
accommodate
achievement
acquaintance
aerial
altogether
amateur
ambiguity
anxious
apparatus
appearance
arguing
auxiliary

basically
beautiful
beneficial
benefited
bicycle
biennial
biscuit
business
buoyant

calendar
catalogue
clothes
committed
committee
colonel
competition
complacent
conscientious
conscious
convalescent

deceived
decrepit
description
definitely

disappointed
disappear
descendant
discipline
dessert
developed

ecstasy
efficient
embarrass
extraordinary
exaggerate
excellent
excitement

fascinate
fatigue
February
foreigner
fulfil

gauge
government
grammar
gregarious
grievance
grievous

handkerchief
harass
hasten
humorous

immediately
inadvertently
independent
incidentally
incongruous
indictment
indispensable
irrelevant

library
laboratory
lieutenant
likeable
likely
liquefied
literature

maintenance
margarine
miscellaneous
mischievous
monotonous
municipal

necessity
necessary
nostalgia
noticeable

occasionally
occurrence
opinion
opportunity
original

parallel
parliament
peculiar
perseverance
personnel
piteous
possession
practical
prejudice
privilege
pronunciation
putrefied

pursuit
purpose

receipt
recognize
recommend

schedule
secretarial
separate
sergeant
sincerely
society
superintendent
supersede
surveyed

taciturn
theatre
transference
transferred
traveller

unanimous
unique
unnatural
unusually

vegetable
veterinary
vicious
vigorously

Wednesday
weird
wholly
written
wrestle
weariness

Get somebody to read about ten words to you at a time from the list, and write them down, checking them for accuracy. Alternatively, you could study three words at a time and then write them down from memory.

JUST FOR FUN

1 Write out the following, putting in the missing letters or words.

(a) A flea and a fly in a flue
Were imprisoned, so what could they do?
Said the fl_, 'Let us fl_.'
Said the fl_, 'Let us fl_.'
So they fl_ through a flaw in the flue.

(b) George the First was always _____
Vile, but viler George the Second.
And what mortal ever _____
Any good of George the Third?
When from earth the Fourth _____,
God be praised, the Georges ended.

(c) tre_____dous   haz_____dous
stu_____dous   hor_____dous
(these are the only common words ending with the letters 'dous')

2 The following sentence (with one word left out) contains all the letters of the alphabet. What is the word that has been left out?

'Jackdaws _____ my big sphinx of quartz.'

3 Add the missing vowels in order to write out the following well-known ten proverbs.
(a) BRDNTHHNDSWRTHTWNTBSH
(b) TMNYCKSSPLTHBRTH
(c) MNYHNDSMKLGHTWRK
(d) STTCHNTMSVSNN
(e) LKBFRYLP
(f) LTSLPNGDGSL

'I have the results of your English examination, and there is good and bad news.'
'Tell me the good news first.'
'You spelled your name right.'

4 What two letters of the alphabet are used most frequently? The answer is 'e' and 't'. Unsure? Well what follows was typed out using the space-bar every time these two letters were required.

Write out the following, putting in the missing letters 'e' and 't'.

My yp wri r works qui w ll xc p for wo k ys.
Som im s i s ms o m ha my
 nglish class is lik my yp wri r; no
all h k ys ar working prop rly.

You migh say o yours lf: 'W ll, I am
only on of h wo s ud n s my
  ach r is hin ing a ; i won' mak
much diff r nc .'

Bu you s for h class o b r ally
 ff c iv and succ d i n ds h
ac iv e par t icipa ion of v ry pupil
pr s n t. So, h n x   im you hink
 ha your ffor t is no n d d,
r m mb r my old yp wri er and say
 o yours lf:

'I am a k y p rson: jus as impor an o
 h class as h wo l   rs '' '' and
'' ''ar   o a yp wri r, and I am
n d d v ry much ind d!'